A Sonnet from Carthage

A Sonnet from Carthage

Garcilaso de la Vega and the New Poetry of Sixteenth-Century Europe

RICHARD HELGERSON

PENN

University of Pennsylvania Press

Philadelphia

Copyright © 2007 University of Pennsylvania Press
Printed in the United States of America on acid-free paper

10 9 8 7 6 5 4 3 2 1

Published by
University of Pennsylvania Press
Philadelphia, Pennsylvania 19104-4112

Library of Congress Cataloging-in-Publication Data
Helgerson, Richard.
A sonnet from Carthage : Garcilaso de la Vega and the new poetry of sixteenth-century
Europe / Richard Helgerson.
        p. cm.
    Includes bibiographical references.
    ISBN-13: 978-0-8122-4004-7
    ISBN-10: 0-8122-4004-9 (cloth : alk. paper)
    1. Vega, Garcilaso de la, 1503–1536—Criticism and interpretation.   2. Spanish
poetry—Classical period, 1500–1700—History and criticism.   3. European poetry—
Renaissance, 1450–1600—History and criticism.   I. Title.
PQ6393.G3 Z64   2007
861'.3 22   2006051494

To Marie-Christine,
first and last

Contents

Preface
Diagnosis for an Essay

When I began writing this essay in July 2005, the role I imagined for it was wholly unlike the role it now takes. It was to have been a chapter in a large comparative study on the self-consciously "new poetry" of sixteenth-century Europe. With frequent looks back at Petrarch and the Greeks and Romans, this book was to have spent much time in sixteenth-century Italy before focusing its greatest energies on Spain, France, and England—the Spain of Juan Boscán and Garcilaso de la Vega, the France of Joachim du Bellay and Pierre de Ronsard, and the England of Sir Philip Sidney and Edmund Spenser.

It was a study worth pursuing. In that century and with those writers, the very place and nature of poetry changed in ways that have had extraordinarily long-lasting consequences. In effect, these new poets, as they called themselves, invented the modern poetry of those three great western European countries and, by extension, most of the rest of Europe as well. Such a study would have taken considerable time and effort. But the time and effort would have been happily rewarded by much new learning I would have had an excuse to take on. During the previous several years, I had begun just such a leisurely course of self-education with an edition and translation of one of the finest and most influential of the new poets, the Frenchman Joachim du Bellay, an edition I completed and sent to its publisher in June just before turning to the Garcilaso chapter, and I was looking forward to many other such wanderings along the way. At that pleasant rate, the five-to-six-year book I was imagining could easily have stretched out to fill decades.

Then on August 23—the day after my sixty-fifth birthday—reality of a harsher sort intervened. My doctor announced that I had an inoperable pancreatic cancer and that, other than securing immediate, specialized medical care, my first job should be setting my affairs in order. With that news, the chapter on Garcilaso came to a stop midsentence and all plans for the book on the "new poetry" ended. Or so I thought. But after getting the chemotherapy going, putting in the needed time with lawyers and benefit counselors, and responding to a great number of generous and encouraging wishes from family and friends—a terminal cancer diagnosis provides, I have discovered, a wonderful opportunity for an extended, slow-motion memorial service *in vivo*—my thoughts began to drift back to Garcilaso. There was, I realized, a reason I had started with him and with the single sonnet that was to be the topic of that chapter.

From the time I had first read the poem some three years earlier, it drew into its orbit with ever increasing power at each new encounter the whole of the new poetry as I had come to know it over many years of reading, writing, and teaching. In a single fourteen-line sonnet, which had not even been included in the earliest collections of Garcilaso's work and which has never emerged as one of his most intensively studied poems, I found expressed the deepest ambitions, longings, reservations, affections, jealousies, disillusionments, and interdependencies that had shaped the new poetry wherever it appeared. In reading Garcilaso's sonnet I heard anew and with a fresher note what I had heard so often in Petrarch, du Bellay, Ronsard, Sidney, and Spenser. And yet Garcilaso and the particular experience out of which he wrote remained irreducibly individual in a poem that deserved attention all on its own. With no chance—barring an utterly improbable medical miracle—of my writing the long and learned study of the new poetry, perhaps, if the cancer allowed me the several months that seem often to be within its largess, I would be able to write a version of that book in the form of an extended essay on Garcilaso and this one sonnet, a sonnet he wrote to his friend Boscán in July 1535 from the fortress of Goleta in the near neighborhood of ancient Carthage, as he took part in the emperor Charles V's triumphant defeat of the Moorish corsair Kheir-ed-Din.

My idea of what such an essay might look like was shaped by a book I picked up as an occasional distraction for those long chemotherapy sessions in the oncology suite, Jared Diamond's *Collapse*. As those who have read that book will remember, Diamond builds his harrowing account of what humankind has done and is still doing to our shared environment out of a series of highly detailed and yet richly suggestive case studies, some present—Montana, Hispaniola, China, Australia, Somalia, Rwanda and Burundi—and some ancient—Easter Island, Pitcairn and Henderson, the Anasazi country of the American Southwest, Mayan Central America, and the Norse lands of the Atlantic, especially Greenland. With less ample time than Diamond had, I could attempt only a single case study. But Garcilaso and his sonnet seemed ideally suited. With its last words—*me deshago*, "I am undone"—his sonnet might almost seem another of Jared Diamond's stories of ultimate collapse. And in some way it is. The great triumph of Charles V's military victory, with which the poem begins, ends with the undoing of the man who was unquestionably the emperor's most sensitively responsive warrior, Garcilaso himself. And that personal undoing had its counterpart in history, as Spain's imperial future failed to realize much of the great destiny that had been imagined for it. What could be more like the stories of overweening ambition and accomplishment Diamond tells and the destructive ends to which they are brought?

Like Diamond's stories, too, this is an ecologically complex one. The making of the new poetry in Spain, as in France and England, was the combined product of large political and cultural transformations of the sort Diamond chronicles so brilliantly in his earlier book, *Guns, Germs, and Steel*, and of the intimately personal needs and desires of the men and women who were caught up in those transformations. From the highest and most abstract level, a level at which individual actors hardly seem to matter at all, to the most immediate, Garcilaso's poem brings together, as do many of Diamond's stories, the large and the small, the barely perceptible "it" and the intensely experiencing "I."

But if in an inescapably manifest way Garcilaso's poem tells a story of collapse, it also and on its own terms participates in a story of triumph. It represents the birth of a new poetry that was to provide its culture with a way of expressing its highest ambitions and its sharpest self-doubts for centuries to come. That I and thousands like me now are, as other thousands have been for the last century and a half, professors of modern literature and that millions of students have passed through our courses and emerged with, we hope, a greater understanding of the languages we share and the human issues that most deeply concern us, is the result of poems like those Garcilaso was writing in the 1530s. Garcilaso's tragedy—the self-immolation to which his poem leads—represents a great triumph of the human spirit, one from which inspiration and hope comparable to those that Diamond finds in at least a few of his stories can spring. The beauty Garcilaso and the other new poets of sixteenth-century Europe brought into being not only sustains us spiritually but also helps us understand why this world of ours is worth saving, even as we realize that the human accomplishments we most treasure have, like Garcilaso's own poem, been tied to some of our most self-destructive perversities.

As a narrative of collapse analogous to the stories Diamond tells, Garcilaso's poem gains force from the very nature of poetry, its movement through time as we read from its first word to its last. In that reading experience, each new revelation has the possibility of reversing what has gone before, with the result that the last word, whatever that last word may be, feels like the last word indeed, like the ultimate discovery—*me deshago*—toward which the poem as a whole has been moving with irre-sistible force.

Yet the analogy is partial, imperfect, even deeply misleading. That is where the counter-story, the story of triumph comes in. Unlike the over-turned, broken, and mutilated statues Diamond finds on Easter Island, unlike the island's now barren landscape and its ravaged population of native flora and fauna and Polynesian invaders, the full imperial con-quest and glory of Garcilaso's poem remain undiminished when the poem ends. Despite its movement in time, a poem is not only a tempo-ral structure, and still less an irreversibly temporal one. As much as it lives in time, a poem also lives in simultaneity. The imperial restoration, the "arms and the fury of Mars," with which Garcilaso begins, persists uncanceled and unchanged even though Garcilaso is himself undone. For as long as the beginning and ending continue to coexist, the poem as a whole endures intact. On this Easter Island, the monumental stat-ues are still standing, the great forests continue to flourish, the native and invading populations remain as numerous and as vigorous as they ever were, even as we simultaneously see and lament their catastrophic loss.

And what is true of Garcilaso's single sonnet, a sonnet that offers as ir-resistibly compelling a narrative movement as I know, is no less true of the new poetry of sixteenth-century Europe as a broad, capacious, and wonderfully enduring literary historical accomplishment. If that poetry shares—as it certainly does—Garcilaso's initially celebratory affiliation with empire, it persists in sharing that commitment even though it also finds itself no less deeply entangled in a Garcilaso-like loss of self, a merging of its poetic voice into the voice of a radical and perhaps ulti-mately transcendent undoing. Even more than Garcilaso's individual poem, the new poetry of sixteenth-century Europe offers a structure of simultaneity. Nor do the extremes of imperial ambition and ultimate self-loss exhaust its commitments. As I will suggest, both Garcilaso's poem and the new poetry as a whole share at least three other deep af-filiations, three other sources of energy and identity, each one of which rivals the others without ever supplanting them. Both Garcilaso's sonnet and the new poetry arise from a dynamically shifting yet remarkably sta-ble foundation of jostling impulses that, in the particularity of any one poetic narrative or any one interpretive exposition, may seem to have successfully displaced the others. But, however compelling those unidi-rectional stories are, they must, like the analogy of Easter Island's col-lapse, be resisted. However compelling any one affiliation or impulse, each depends finally on its mutual adherence to the others.

That I should make Garcilaso—and still more a single, relatively neg-lected sonnet of his—carry the weight of this large literary historical argument may seem grossly disproportionate, even to devoted students of the sixteenth century. Like virtually all Hispanic literature prior to the emergence in the last century of figures such as Pablo Neruda, Jorge Luis Borges, Gabriel García Márquez, and Carlos Fuentes—with, of course, the towering exception of Cervantes' *Don Quixote*—Garcilaso and the other writers of Renaissance Spain are thought of, when they are thought of at all, as little more than distant echoes of their Italian, French, and English contemporaries. The geographical and linguistic marginality of Spain, as compared particularly with Italy and France, kept them from achieving full recognition beyond the Iberian peninsula in their own time, and the centuries-long political, military, and economic decline of Spain, which first became unmistakable around 1600, has kept them far from the center of literary-historical consciousness ever since.

And yet, rightly considered, Garcilaso deserves far more than the preeminent position he securely holds in the literary history of Spain, deserves a more fully European reputation. Together with his friend Juan Boscán, he is every bit the Spanish counterpart of Joachim du Bellay and Pierre de Ronsard in France and of Sir Philip Sidney and Edmund Spenser in England. Indeed, he and Boscán are the forerunners of those French and English poets, for their radical remaking of Spanish poetry in imitation of the poets of modern Italy and ancient Rome predates du Bellay and Ronsard's remaking of French poetry along similar lines by a full decade and a half and anticipates the laggardly Sidney and Spenser by half a century. And where in France and England both of the men most closely identified with the founding of this innovative new poetry—both du Bellay and Ronsard, both Sidney and Spenser—have retained a strong following, in Spain Garcilaso soon emerged as the single dominant figure, "the prince of Spanish poets," as he has been repeatedly called since the middle years of the sixteenth century.

Garcilaso's dominance was not immediately apparent. His poems and Boscán's were first published together in 1543—seven years after the death of Garcilaso and six months after the death of Boscán—in an edition entitled *Las obras de Boscán y algunas de Garcilaso de la Vega, repartidas en quatro libros*—*The Works of Boscán and Some by Garcilaso de la Vega, Distributed in Four Books*. Not only did Boscán get top billing, but three of the four books were filled with his poems. There were good reasons for this preference. The older Boscán seems at least at first to have been the leading partner in their innovative departure, and it was he who in the introduction to the second book of the collection—a collection he assembled and that his widow brought to completion and had printed in Boscán's hometown of Barcelona—wrote the manifesto defining for the reading public what he and Garcilaso had done and proclaiming its superiority to all previous Spanish poetry. Furthermore, as the Spanish translator of Castiglione's *Book of the Courtier*—a task Garcilaso had prompted him to undertake and had joined in presenting—Boscán had a more public literary reputation. And he had, in fact, written far more verse. So for the next twenty-five years, through some dozen and a half printings in cities as widely spread as Lisbon, Antwerp, Lyon, Paris, Valladolid, Venice, Estella, and Toledo, Garcilaso's poems appeared as an appendage to the work of his more renowned friend.

But all that changed in 1569 when the Salamancan bookseller Simón Borgoñón brought out a corrected edition of Garcilaso alone. From that point on, the combined edition lost its audience and Boscán virtually disappeared from circulation—the first edition of his poems alone was not to come out until 1875—while the poems of Garcilaso took a very different course. First in 1574 there appeared a much augmented edition—now including for the first time the sonnet that is to be the subject of this essay—accompanied by extensive annotations by the Salamancan professor of rhetoric Francisco Sánchez de la Bronzes—better known as El Brocense—and then in 1580 in Seville was published the massive *Obras de Garcilaso de la Vega con anotaciones de Fernando de Herrera*—*The Works of Garcilaso de la Vega with Annotations by Fernando de Herrera*. If ever an edition proclaimed the equality of a near-contemporary vernacular writer to the great poets of modern Italy and of classical Greece and Rome—poets like Homer, Virgil, Horace, Ovid, Petrarch, and Ariosto—this one did. With its extensive notes on each poem, its lengthy essay on each separate genre, its life of Garcilaso, its collection of commendatory poems, and its trumpeting introduction by Herrera's friend and fellow Andalusian poet, Francisco de Medina, this book, whatever ulterior motives it may reveal concerning Herrera's own self-promotion, left no doubt that Garcilaso had lifted Spanish poetry and the Spanish language to the level of the great poetries and great languages of ancient and modern Europe.

What exactly that accomplishment meant, as understood by Medina and Herrera, is the starting place for my first chapter, the chapter entitled "What They Expected (. . . and What They Got)." But because such expectations were so deeply embedded in a tradition that reached back to Rome and was then powerfully renewed in the fourteenth century by Petrarch and his humanist followers, before reaching its early modern culmination in sixteenth-century Italy, Spain, Portugal, France, and England, I relate the claims of Medina and Herrera to similar claims made elsewhere. My main evidence in that regard is the work of those poets who most boldly sought to realize such claims: Virgil and Horace, Petrarch, Ariosto, Pietro Bembo, and Torquato Tasso, du Bellay and Ronsard, Luís de Camões, and Sidney and Spenser. If Garcilaso's sonnet on the imperial reconquest of Tunis is obsessed with memories of Rome, so too are both the praises Medina and Herrera lavish on him and the poetic works, especially the heroic poems among them, that follow self-consciously in the wake of Virgil and his celebration of Rome's imperial destiny.

But this chapter on "what they expected" makes place too for "what they got," for the *me deshago* that Medina and Herrera were less ready to acknowledge in Garcilaso, a *me deshago* that in the figures of Circe, Dido, and their descendants is as much a part of the heroic tradition—a tradition from Virgil on of self-consciously new poetry, poetry of imperial translation and radical cultural self-transformation—as is its triumphant, all-conquering antagonist. In doing so, the chapter specifies in an initial way, later to be complicated still further in the reading of Garcilaso's sonnet, the rival impulses that shaped the new poetry and competed for command of its deepest and most enduring identity.

Once having introduced in however abbreviated and summary a way the expectations and counterexpectations with which Garcilaso and his poem are so fully engaged, I finally turn to the poem itself in five chapters, each of which takes as its title a phrase from the poem: "*Las armas y el furor de Marte /* Arms and the fury of Mars" from the first quatrain; "*El arte italïano /* Italian art" from the second quatrain; "*Aquí /* Here" from the first tercet; "*Me deshago /* I am undone" from the final tercet; and "*Boscán /* Boscán" from the opening word of address. Though these chapters do not strictly confine themselves to the formal unit in which they find their titles, they do follow a certain progression through the poem, until with the chapter on Boscán they jump back to the poem's addressee and its first word. But despite this generally temporal and narrative order, simultaneity rather than progression governs my understanding of both Garcilaso's poem and the new poetry it so richly represents. For each of these chapters takes up an engagement, an affiliation, a commitment, an impulse, a desire that retains its full force in the face of all the others.

I have already said something of the imperial engagement inherited from Rome that belongs to "Arms and the fury of Mars" and the Circean longing for radical transformation and self-loss that underlies "Me deshago." The other claims deserve and will receive no less attention. These are the claim of an almost equally self-alienating and transformative art in "El arte italïano," the claim of a specificity of place (including in Garcilaso's sonnet Carthage itself) that might be overrun by universalist empire and yet provided affiliations empire was powerless to satisfy in "Aquí," and in "Boscán" the claim of male friendship out of which so much of the new poetry of sixteenth-century Europe, not only that of Garcilaso and Boscán, arose.

At its most doctrinaire this essay asserts that those five engagements constitute a whole, each of whose parts is as essential to the underlying Pan-European enterprise as is any of the others. In the epilogue, I renew that assertion with a necessary qualification. Most simply, the qualification is that the new poetry is as much an early modern undertaking as it is one belonging to the Renaissance. In Garcilaso's sonnet we find one of the birthplaces of modernity but also one of the places where modernity encounters ancient doubt.

An essay that takes as its subject both a single sonnet and a literary movement that spread over many countries and many languages necessarily shuttles repeatedly from the one poem to many, from a single sonnet to a body of writing that features most prominently poems that have in their various homelands taken the place of Homer in Greece and Virgil in Rome as central texts of national literary education and even of national self-understanding. But in my reading of Garcilaso's sonnet I also pay frequent attention to his own full poetic corpus and especially to the five other poems he wrote during the year and a half that he was involved with Charles V's Tunis expedition. So important to my understanding of the sonnet are these other "Tunisian" poems that I reprint all five in their original languages—four of them in Spanish and one in Latin—with a facing English translation and some necessary explanatory notes in a brief anthology appended to the essay itself. On its own, each of these poems made a major contribution to the new poetry of sixteenth-century Spain. Together they provide a still fuller demonstration of the five fundamental engagements that underlie and enable both Garcilaso's sonnet from Carthage and the new poetry of sixteenth-century Europe generally.

Before I turn to the chapter on "what they expected," let me make one last and still larger claim. Though this essay concerns a very specific place and time, its implications reach well beyond those limits, reach to efforts at self-conscious literary renewal wherever and whenever they have occurred. The most obvious of those extensions, included within the essay itself, are back to Roman antiquity and to the fourteenth century of Petrarch's Italy. But they also extend forward. The five fundamental conditions I find working through Garcilaso's sonnet and through the new poetry of sixteenth-century Europe—(1) a political transformation needing a new literary expression, (2) a set of formal literary innovations responding to those changes, (3) a commitment to a particular place that sometimes challenges the grander designs of imperial politics, (4) a loss of self in desires that may arise from but often counter political ambition, and (5) the intimately immediate relations between the writers who collectively assume the task of radical literary change—have in different mixes and with different emphases recurred again and again.

As a student of English literature, I think especially of examples from that tradition, though a similar list could readily be compiled from many countries and many languages. But from English alone, consider the Glorious Revolution of 1688 and the generation of Defoe, Swift, Addison, and Steele; Wordsworth, Coleridge, and the later Romantics in the era of the French Revolution; the self-conscious efforts of Emerson, Thoreau, Hawthorne, Melville, Whitman, and Poe to find a literary language for the new American republic; Eliot, Pound, and their generation in a post-Victorian, transatlantic time and space; Lowell, Ginsberg, Berryman, Levertov, Sexton, and Plath in a postwar world of rapid and disruptive change. Consider, too, the still more recent proliferation of new literatures arising from newly self-conscious minority communities in the United States and from regions far removed from the traditional British and American homelands of English literature, from the Caribbean, Australia, South Asia, and various parts of the African continent, including West Africa, where a little over forty years ago I had the fortunate opportunity to begin my own teaching career. I have no idea whether the French and English writers I first read then—Camara Laye, Mongo Beti, Chinua Achebe, Wole Soyinka, Cyprian Ekwensi, and from the other side of the continent James Ngugi (better known since as Ngugi wa Thiong'o)—would recognize anything of their experience in the experience of Garcilaso and his contemporaries, but at its most ambitious this essay does mean to issue such an invitation. And, at the very least, I can testify that my own understanding of sixteenth-century literature has been repeatedly enriched by the years I spent in then newly independent West Africa. Through the lens of such later literary movements, the dramatically innovative renewal of sixteenth-century poetry to which Garcilaso contributed so much reveals its profoundest meaning.

Part I
A Sonnet from Carthage

Soneto a Boscán desde la Goleta

Boscán, las armas y el furor de Marte,
que con su propria fuerça el africano
suelo regando, hazen que el romano
imperio reverdezca en esta parte,
    han reduzido a la memoria el arte
y el antiguo valor italïano,
por cuya fuerça y valerosa mano
Africa se aterró de parte a parte.
    Aquí donde el romano encendimiento,
dond' el fuego y la llama licenciosa
solo el nombre dexaron a Cartago,
    buelve y rebuelve amor mi pensamiento,
hiere y enciend' el alma temerosa,
y en llanto y en ceniza me deshago.

Sonnet to Boscán from Goleta

Boscán, arms and the fury of Mars, which, watering the African soil with
its own strength, make the Roman Empire flourish once again in this
region,

have led back to memory the art and ancient Italian valor by whose
strength and valorous hand Africa was leveled from end to end.

Here, where the Roman conflagration, where fire and licentious flame
left only the name of Carthage,

love turns and turns again my thought, wounds and inflames my fearful
soul, and in tears and ashes I am undone.

What They Expected
(... and What They Got)

"It has always been the natural intent of a victorious people to endeavor to spread the use of its language at least as far as the limits of its empire." These are the opening words of Francisco de Medina's introduction to Fernando de Herrera's massive annotated edition of *The Works of Garcilaso de la Vega*, the book that, as I have said, did most to define for sixteenth-century Spaniards the meaning of Garcilaso's poetic accomplishment. Penciled at this point into the margin of my university library's facsimile copy of Herrera is the name "Nebrija." The connection is obvious and right. In 1492, just a month after Ferdinand and Isabella completed the centuries-long reconquest of the Iberian peninsula with their defeat of the last Moorish stronghold of Granada and a few months before Columbus returned from his voyage across the Atlantic, the leading Spanish humanist Antonio de Nebrija presented his *Castilian Grammar*, the first grammar of a European vernacular, to Queen Isabella with the ringing declaration that "language has always been the companion of empire"—*siempre la lengua fue compañera del imperio*. The problem for Nebrija, a problem his grammar was intended to address, was that the Spanish language was not yet ready to assume the place at empire's side that the great languages of antiquity—Hebrew, Greek, and Latin—had once filled. Empire might be at hand, but Spanish still needed work.

Now, eighty-eight years later, Medina echoes Nebrija to announce that, though there is still much to be done, Garcilaso's poetry stands as proof that the language of Spain is up to the task. Garcilaso has, as Medina puts it, "clearly shown how much the strength of an excellent Spanish talent can accomplish and that it is not impossible for our language to reach the height where Greek and Latin are already to be seen." Following Garcilaso's example, we will, Medina suggests, be able to rescue this language from ignorance and barbarity. "From now on, the arrogance and presumption of the common herd will shrink, for they, deceived by a false sense of their entitlement, dared boldly kidnap this most honest of matrons, expecting her to surrender at their first bidding, as if she were a vile and shameless whore. May men of talent be stirred to enter this glorious contest, and we will see the majesty of the Spanish language, arrayed with new and admirable splendor, spread to the farthest territories where the standards of our armies will victoriously penetrate." Thanks to Garcilaso, the Spanish language, the erstwhile plaything of the vulgar masses, can truly be made, as Nebrija desired, a worthy companion of a militant, aristocratic, and expanding empire.

These extraordinary claims may seem to border on the absurd. What dependence can imperial conquest have on poetry, particularly on the kind of lyric poetry Garcilaso wrote? That Garcilaso had himself been a companion not only of empire but also of the emperor did, however, lend such claims a certain credibility. Named as a member of Charles V's personal guard in 1520, Garcilaso was in the emperor's company sixteen years later when he suffered the wounds from which he died. In the intervening decade and a half, he received many signs of imperial favor and performed many acts of imperial service. In 1523, he was initiated into the Order of Santiago—Charles invested him personally—and was knighted. In 1525, he was married to Elena de Zúñiga, a lady-in-waiting to the emperor's sister Eleanor of Austria, who, along with the emperor, supplied a large part of the bride's generous dowry. In 1535, he was appointed chatelain of the Italian city of Reggio, and in 1536, was given command of three thousand soldiers in the army Charles was assembling to retake Savoy and invade the south of France. And during those same years, he took part in expeditions against the *comuneros* uprising in his native Castile, against the Turkish menace in Rhodes, against the French in the Pyrenees, against the Turks in Vienna and later in North Africa, where he wrote the sonnet that is the principal subject of this essay. Nor was his service only military. He twice represented the imperial court in embassies concerning Eleanor of Austria's marriage to King Francis I, joined the emperor in his first voyage to Italy, and repeatedly served as a distinguished messenger between the emperor and Don Pedro de Toledo, the emperor's viceroy in Naples. As deeply as ideas of empire permeate the new poetry of sixteenth-century Europe—not only in Spain but also in Italy, France, Portugal, and England—no other sixteenth-century poet, certainly none of comparable stature, had so long and so intimate a connection with the actual workings of imperial warfare and diplomacy. Thinking, as Medina and Herrera obviously do, of Garcilaso as a great poet of empire, a poet whose reform of Spanish verse served the same ends as his military and political employment, would thus appear all but irresistible, whatever the nature of the poems Garcilaso actually wrote. The part of imperial poet had already been clearly scripted by Nebrija and many others. Who but Garcilaso had better played it?

This union of arms and letters is nicely illustrated on the frontispiece Herrera designed for his edition. Here we see the warrior's helmet resting on the poet's book surrounded by the oak leaves of military victory and the laurel wreath of poetic accomplishment, the whole ringed by a Latin inscription declaring that Garcilaso was "no less eminent in this than in that." That double identity as soldier and poet has remained central to the image of Garcilaso ever since. The two most recent Spanish biographies are suggestively titled *Garcilaso de la Vega: Between Verse and Sword* (1992) and *Garcilaso: Poet of Love, Knight of War* (2002). But the Nebrijan companionship of empire and language finds even more adamant expression on the frontispiece of the very first edition of Garcilaso's poetry, where in 1543 it was printed in tandem with the works of his friend Juan Boscán. There, with no specific reference to the poets and their particular qualities, the book is simply stamped with the imperial arms of Charles V, the double-headed Habsburg eagle, the pillars of Hercules, and the emperor's familiar motto *Plus ultra*—"Yet beyond." In these years many books of many sorts appeared with the same mark of imperial privilege. But that in no way lessens the underlying message. All language, including the language of poetry, emanates from and belongs to the imperial state. By their very use of the language, Garcilaso and Boscán are of necessity made the companions of empire.

Yet, in Garcilaso's case, despite all the evidence of actual imperial favor and service and despite the subsequent understanding of his role as soldier and poet, there remain undeniable signs of tension between him and Charles V's imperial regime. Most obvious are his family connections. At the very moment when Garcilaso first entered the emperor's service, his older brother, Pedro Laso, one of the early leaders of what became the *comuneros* revolt, was distinguishing himself as the most eloquent and one of the most outspoken opponents of the young, foreign, and newly enthroned ruler's policies in Spain. For this opposition, Pedro Laso was exiled to Gibraltar and denied the monarch's favor. Nor did Garcilaso himself wholly escape reproach. In 1531, his attendance at the marriage of his namesake and nephew, Pedro's son—a marriage the empress was intent on preventing—provoked her anger, and that anger was inflamed when Garcilaso's answers to an official interrogation were far from conciliatory. As a result, he was exiled from Spain and for a time confined by order of the emperor to an island in the Danube. But perhaps even more striking is the lack of any poem by Garcilaso addressed to the emperor. Indeed, so far as we can tell, Charles V did not even know that his officer was a poet. Letters from Don Pedro de Toledo to the emperor recommending Garcilaso for preferment speak warmly of his ability and devotion but say nothing of any literary accomplishments, though, as the dedicatee of Garcilaso's first eclogue, Don Pedro was unusually well placed to know what a fine poet he was. And Garcilaso's own single surviving letter to the emperor talks about troop movements in the region of Genoa but makes no mention of poetry. The poet's companionship with empire seems thus not to have included his poems, at least not so far as the emperor knew.

Now there is perhaps nothing very surprising about this. Unlike the kings of England and France, Charles was not particularly known for his interest in good letters, especially not in Spanish, a language he learned only after becoming king of Spain. And we could hardly expect a commander to mention verse in a military dispatch to his sovereign. Nor do the issues that at various moments set Garcilaso and his family against the emperor necessarily reveal a more general disaffection. But, still, when we read Garcilaso's poetry in the light of the full range of his experience, it is hard not to notice a split between the project of poetry and the project of empire. And given the similarity of the literary and political undertakings of Garcilaso and of Charles V to what was happening elsewhere in Europe in the course of the sixteenth century, the split we find here may have broader implications. For not only in Spain did expectations like Nebrija's shape the production and reception of the new poetry. Not only in Spain did consolidation at home and expansion abroad revive dreams of universal empire. And not only in Spain did such dreams draw attention to the insufficiency of the national vernacular and its literature. The role that was scripted in advance for Garcilaso and that determined the way his accomplishment was understood was as readily available in Italy, France, Portugal, and England as in Spain.

For what is no doubt the most militantly outspoken expression of those ambitions, we need look no further than to a book published in Paris just six years after the appearance of the joint edition of Boscán's and Garcilaso's poems, Joachim du Bellay's *Deffence et illustration de la langue françoyse—The Defense and Enrichment of the French Language*. Like Medina and Herrera and like Nebrija before them, du Bellay is prompted by a sense, as he puts it, that the time is fast approaching "when this noble and powerful kingdom will in its turn seize the reins of universal dominion." But like them, he worries about the barbarity of his native language, its inadequacy as a companion of empire. His solution—very much the solution Nebrija had already proposed for Spanish and that Boscán and Garcilaso had realized in their poetry—was to do to French what he understood Cicero, Virgil, Horace, and Ovid had done to Latin in the moment of Rome's great expansion and imperial efflorescence—that is, to remake it in imitation of a language or of languages that had already attained the requisite degree of refinement. As the Romans had imitated the Greeks, so the French should imitate the

Greeks, the Romans, and the modern Italians, who with Petrarch and Boccaccio had already remade their vernacular. And if this meant turning one's back on all previous writing in French, so be it. To be made fit for empire, French would have to be made foreign. Thus from ancient Rome through the humanist revival of fourteenth-century Italy to the various vernaculars of sixteenth-century Europe, the new poetry was always a poetry of deliberate and radical self-estrangement, a poetry that abandoned the self to become another.

To undertake such a project required powerful motivation. The dream of universal empire—a dream that for the Romans and at least some of their sixteenth-century successors had a firm basis in political and military reality—supplied it. In the Roman case, the transformation of a pastoral village into the *caput mundi*—the head of the world—was so undeniably spectacular that it put an inescapable pressure on Rome's literary culture. "Can anyone be so indifferent or idle," wrote Polybius, "as not to care to know by what means and under what kind of polity almost the whole inhabited world was conquered and brought under the dominion of the single city of Rome, and that within a period of not quite fifty-three years?" A historian like Polybius had one way of responding to this astounding accomplishment. Poets like Virgil and Horace had another. But the magnitude of the accomplishment, which included the conquest of both the highly cultivated lands of the eastern Mediterranean and North Africa and the barbarous lands of the west, Iberia, Gaul, and eventually Britain, could not be ignored and required that the arts of war and government be joined by the more peaceful arts the Romans learned from their newly subjected peoples, including most obviously the Greeks. As a result, Latin prose and Latin verse were both remade in imitation of Greek models. Greek rhetoric, Greek philosophy, Greek genres, Greek metrics, Greek mythology, and even Greek words supplanted their crude Latin rivals. As Horace put it, "Captive Greece took her fierce conqueror captive and introduced her arts into rude Latium." Could ordinary, unlearned Romans comprehend the essentially alien work that arose from this capture? Scholars have wondered. But clearly Horace and his fellow Augustan poets, like Cicero in the last years of the Republic, felt that Rome's unprecedented expansion demanded the wholesale adoption of superior, though foreign, ways of writing.

Some fifteen hundred years later it was the turn of the barbarian provinces Rome had once conquered—Iberia, now divided into the kingdoms of Spain and Portugal; Gaul, now renamed France; and Britain, now dominated by the kingdom of England—to experience or at least to imagine for themselves an expansion comparable to Rome's and to feel the need, as Nebrija and du Bellay both did, to render their

homely vernaculars as artful and as illustrious as the languages of
Greece and Rome. The union of the kingdoms of Aragon and Castile,
the conquest of Granada, the spread of Spanish power into the New
World, the continued control of Sardinia and Sicily, the acquisition of
the kingdom of Naples and much of the kingdom of Navarre already
gave proof under Ferdinand and Isabella of Spain's growing strength.
And when in 1516 their grandson Charles of Ghent inherited the Spanish crowns, he brought with him large territories in the Netherlands and
Burgundy to which he soon added the widespread German and Austrian lands of the Holy Roman Empire, made available by the death in
1519 of his other grandfather, Maximilian I. Here, indeed, was an empire fit to recall the greatness of Rome. And following on its own "reconquest" from the Moors and its vast maritime expansion from Brazil,
around the coast of Africa, to India and the Far East, Spain's Iberian
neighbor, Portugal, entertained similar thoughts, as did the rapidly expanding and consolidating kingdom of France, whose armies invaded
Italy in 1494 and whose king competed with Charles for the imperial
crown. Nor were they alone. Even England, "cut off from all the world,"
as Virgil had said of the Britons in his first eclogue, declared itself "an
empire" and schemed to extend its sway beyond neighboring Ireland to
the northern reaches of the New World and farther still.

For the Spanish, the Portuguese, the French, and the English, the way
to the new learning and the new vernacular poetry that imperial accomplishment demanded passed through Italy. Italian humanism defined
the curriculum of the schools in which poets like Garcilaso, Boscán, du
Bellay, Ronsard, Camões, Sidney, and Spenser were formed. Italian writing—books like Lorenzo Valla's *On the Elegances of the Latin Language*,
Baldesar Castiglione's *Book of the Courtier*, Pietro Bembo's *Prose Pieces on
the Vulgar Tongue*, and Sperone Speroni's *Dialogue on Languages*—drew
attention to the question of language and poetic style. And most often
Italian poetry, especially the vernacular poetry of Petrarch and his sixteenth-century followers, provided the new poets with their first models.
Garcilaso and Boscán started there, and so did du Bellay, Camões, and
Sidney. And if Ronsard gave priority to the Pindaric ode and Spenser to
the Virgilian eclogue, both soon found their way to Petrarch and the
sonnet sequence.

But what of the Italians themselves? Their situation was the reverse of
what prompted the Spanish, Portuguese, French, and English. Far from
experiencing national consolidation and territorial expansion, they
knew only division and defeat. Unmistakable loss thus defined the Italian attitude toward both language and poetry. What had been—that is,
a world empire centered in Italy—was no more and gave little sign of
staging a return. Yet in loss the preoccupation with empire was no less

intense for the Italians than it was for their more fortunate neighbors to the west. If anything, that preoccupation was more intense, and it certainly arose earlier. Already in the fourteenth century, Petrarch was driven as both scholar and poet by a desire to see Rome flourish once more in Italy, a desire that found political expression in his enthusiastic support for Cola di Rienzo's ill-fated attempt to revive the Roman republic, his subsequent effort to entice Charles IV to transfer his imperial court from Prague to Rome and to attend more to the interests of Italy, and his repeated lamentations at the subjection of Rome to the papal curia in Avignon. And if such political initiatives failed, as they always did, Petrarch could at least give Rome and Italy a poet worthy of empire. A laureate coronation, like the one conferred on Petrarch in 1341 by the Roman senate, would, with the Latin and Italian works that justified that coronation, have to take the place of any more concrete imperial revival. Lacking its imperial companion, language kept at least a phantom of an Italian-based empire alive.

The idea that restored Latinity or perhaps even a newly refined Italian vernacular—in both of which Petrarch led the way—could serve as a surrogate for lost and seemingly irrecoverable imperial power persisted from the fourteenth century well into the sixteenth, when French and Spanish invasions, culminating, though not ending, with the notorious imperial sack of Rome in 1527, made Italy's position still more abject than it had been when Petrarch wrote. Listen, for example, to a voice from the intervening fifteenth century, a voice that continued to resonate for a century and more. Here is Lorenzo Valla in the preface to his enormously influential *On the Elegances of the Latin Language*. "Subject peoples may have thrown off the yoke of Roman arms, but they remain under the yoke of the Latin language. . . . Italy, France, Spain, Germany . . . and many other countries are still ours. Wherever the language of Rome dominates, the Roman Empire lives on." Particularly worth noting is Valla's possessive "ours." Like Petrarch before him and scores of Italian humanists after him, Valla identifies with the Roman Empire. The continuing predominance of the language of Rome, a language Valla was working to renew, belonged to Valla himself. In similar fashion, sixteenth-century Italians looked to linguistic refinement, whether in Latin or in the vernacular, as an antidote to the continuing humiliation and subjection of their divided homeland. Castiglione defends his use of words from his native Lombard on grounds that, having remained closer to Latin than those of other Italian dialects, including Tuscan, they "have kept their dignity and splendor, when, by way of the wars and ruins of Italy, changes have come about in the language, in the buildings, dress, and customs." Though arguing for the very Tuscan Castiglione dismisses, Bembo in his *Prose Pieces* similarly evokes the "injuries of enemy nations and time" as the condition to be remedied by cultivation of the Italian vernacular. And Speroni stages his debate between defenders of classical Latin, fourteenth-century Tuscan, and current courtly usage against the background of imperial aspiration and loss. Whatever preeminence Italy retains in the midst of political and military ruin derives from linguistic superiority. "We live and talk with barbarians," Speroni has the Bembo who appears as one of the interlocutors in his *Dialogue* say, "without becoming barbarian."

No wonder then that the "barbarians" themselves—the modern Iberians, Gauls, and Britons—encountering such views would have felt compelled to give their own vernaculars a refinement comparable to that of Latin and modern Italian. That they did in fact repeatedly have such encounters is beyond question. Nebrija was a close student of Valla and got his notion of the companionship of language and empire from the prefaces to the several books of Valla's *Elegances*. Boscán knew Castiglione in Spain and translated *The Book of the Courtier*. Garcilaso lived among Italian humanists and poets in Naples and corresponded with Bembo. Du Bellay borrowed large chunks of his *Defense* from Speroni and wrote his best poetry in Rome. Sidney also visited Italy, and Spenser was inspired by the rousing response his teacher, Richard Mulcaster, made on behalf of the English vernacular to claims like Valla's: "For is it not indeed a marvelous bondage to become servants to one tongue for learning sake . . . whereas we may have the very same treasure in our own tongue, . . . our own bearing the joyful title of liberty and freedom, the Latin tongue remembering us of our thralldom and bondage?" And, of course, they all read and imitated Petrarch.

Such imitation was crucial. The way out of bondage and barbarism—and remember that with the Moorish occupation of Spain and Portugal, the fourteenth- and fifteenth-century English triumphs in France, and the Norman and papal yokes borne by England itself, each of these countries had suffered foreign overlordship since the fall of Rome—was through a proclamation of absolute sovereignty that depended on possession of a vernacular capable of the artful expression that Cicero, Virgil, and Horace had achieved for Latin and that Petrarch, Boccaccio, and Bembo managed for Italian. That seems to be what Spenser has in mind when he hails du Bellay as the "first garland of free Poësie / That France brought forth" and what Medina and Herrera celebrate in the accomplishment of Garcilaso. From this perspective, freedom, empire, and literary refinement can only be fully enjoyed together. With neither freedom nor empire, the Italians had to make do with ancient memories and a modern refinement that replicated what Rome had once known. Without refinement, the Spanish, Portuguese, French, and English, prior to the emergence of the new poets, still fell short of humanist expectation despite their growing claim on both freedom and empire. Joining refinement in the national vernacular to the accomplishments of arms and government was the way to satisfy an expectation that never stopped thinking of Rome.

This, in the view of Medina and Herrera, is what Garcilaso had done for Spain, what later commentators would claim Ronsard and du Bellay had done for France, what Camões had done for Portugal, what Sidney and Spenser had done for England. But in these proclamations of success in the great task of equaling the poetic refinement of the Greeks and Latins, there is, especially in the reception of Garcilaso, a curious indifference to the actual content of the poems themselves. Their artful, imported formal features, their alien metrics, generic forms, figures, tropes, and even diction, are clearly of the greatest importance and receive admiring and extended attention. Indisputable marks of the much-desired and hitherto lacking poetic elevation, these formal features make Garcilaso's Spanish a fit companion for empire. But it seems not to matter at all that the poems, which are destined, as Medina puts it, to accompany the victorious armies of Spain to the farthest reaches of the known world, speak mainly of frustration, loss, self-alienation, and even self-immolation. Can this be the voice of imperial triumph, the voice of the new Rome?

Already in glancing at Garcilaso's biography, we noticed a possible split between the project of poetry and the project of empire. Here that split would seem to expand to an unbridgeable gulf. Yet neither Medina nor Herrera shows the least inclination to acknowledge the existence of such a gulf. As his sonnet from Carthage and the other poems he wrote in the course of the Tunis expedition make clear, Garcilaso was not so oblivious. Nor were the other new poets from Virgil and Petrarch through their sixteenth-century Italian, French, Portuguese, and English followers. On the contrary, the conflict between imperial ambition and other less easily admitted desires remained their single most persistent preoccupation. And nowhere is that conflict more apparent than in the poems that set out most deliberately, as Garcilaso's rarely do, to make the triumphs of empire their central subject. These are the poems, the epics and heroic romances that descend from Virgil's *Aeneid*—Petrarch's *Africa*, Ariosto's *Orlando furioso*, Ronsard's *Franciade*, Camões's *Lusiads*, Tasso's *Jerusalem Delivered*, Sidney's *Arcadia*, Spenser's *Faerie Queene*, and some closely related lyrical works by du Bellay and Giordano Bruno—we need to recall, however briefly, if we are to appreciate how deeply Garcilaso's sonnet from Carthage is entangled in the issues that trouble the new poetry wherever it emerges.

Fulfilling this mandate will inevitably involve something of a romp through fifteen hundred years of literary history and the work of a dozen poets in just a few pages. Given the uneven familiarity of readers with the ten or so epics and heroic romances I shall be mentioning, this could lead to considerable cognitive overload, if not just plain confusion. These are big poems, and not many people keep the details of more than a few of them in their heads at any one time. But despite the plethora of only semifamiliar facts, the large outline of my argument should be clear. Whatever their devotion to empire, these epics inevitably run into moments of erotic enchantment that both threaten their imperial mission and provide an often unavoidable alternative to the poetry of empire. The narrative results vary widely, from total repudiation and harsh retribution to the embrace of sensual distraction as a step on the way to a greater poetic and even imperial fulfillment. But all through the tradition, tensions run deep and are only rarely, if ever, resolved in a way that adequately acknowledges the full claims of each side. That is the very nature of the new poetry as it descended from Rome to Garcilaso and to the other poets of sixteenth-century Europe. Theirs is a poetry of profound self-division.

Virgil himself provides an obvious example. Certainly no one could miss the imperial engagement of the *Aeneid*. From the divine promise in book 1 that the descendants of Aeneas will be "lords of the world" to Aeneas's decisive victory over Turnus in book 12, the poem is resolutely bent on enlisting Greek art, the art of the Homeric epic, in the service of Augustan rule. But even the *Aeneid*, in the episode of Aeneas's love affair with the passionate and tragically doomed Carthaginian queen Dido, imagines an alternative to Rome's imperial destiny, one that early modern readers found irresistibly attractive. When in the 1540s Henry Howard, the earl of Surrey, anticipated England's venture in new poetry with his "strange" innovation of blank verse, he did so by translating the Dido episode from Virgil, and a decade later Joachim du Bellay chose the same episode, to which he added Dido's epistle to Aeneas from Ovid's *Heroides* and an epigram of Ausonius "declaring the truth concerning the story of Dido," to show off the newly acquired power of French verse. For both Surrey and du Bellay, Dido and her story trump the appeal of even Aeneas and his. And whether they take Dido as their model or go back to the still more literally enchanting and more menacing Circe of Homer's *Odyssey*, each of the new poets who attempts a work of heroic ambition, a work that renews something of Virgil's imperial design, finds himself and his poem caught up in desires that threaten the very imperial identity he has set out to affirm.

The original Circe makes men forget their country and transforms them into swine. Spenser's Acrasia in book 2 of *The Faerie Queene* has a similar effect on the men who succumb to her beauty. She must thus be taken captive and her Bower of Bliss must be destroyed, an act Spenser's

knight of temperance performs with a violence and a relentless zeal—
"And of the fairest late, now made the fowlest place"—that only magni-
fies the attraction of what must be sacrificed if empire is to succeed. In
reading Spenser on the destruction of the Bower of Bliss, as in reading
Virgil on Dido's suicide, it is hard not to feel that poetry here turns
against itself, that what is lost matters more than what is gained. And
that feeling is, if anything, still stronger in *Jerusalem Delivered*, where
Tasso's ostensible devotion to Goffredo and his God-given mission of
uniting the Christian forces assembled around Jerusalem into an "empire of the Holy Lands," an eleventh-century foreshadowing of the ideal
Counter-Reformation state, is opposed by an irrepressible longing for
romance and adventure. Though Tasso does all he can to give his
Circean episode, the captivity of the Christian warrior Rinaldo by the pagan sorceress Armida, an unequivocal moral significance, he seems finally no more able than Rinaldo to resist seduction. Like Virgil's Dido,
Tasso's Armida emerges as the poem's most complex and compelling
figure, and he, like Spenser describing the Bower of Bliss, lavishes on
Armida's Fortunate Isle the most exquisite excesses of his poetic art.
Nor are these resemblances accidental. Armida's passionate outburst at
Rinaldo's departure comes directly from Dido's rage and despair at Aeneas's betrayal, while Spenser borrows from Tasso much of the sensuous
language that adorns his Bower. And between Homer and Virgil at one
end of this tradition of erotic enchantment and Tasso and Spenser at
the other comes still another such scene, one that attracted enormous
critical and poetic attention in the sixteenth century, the sensual enthrallment of the destined hero Ruggiero by the Circean Alcina, an
episode from *Orlando furioso* that Ariosto and even more his host of commentators wrapped in a thick protective veil of moral allegory. But for
all their efforts, there remains a sense that Ariosto's poem, like those of
his predecessors and successors, is most truly itself in this moment of
erotic self-abandonment. Certainly Ruggiero's enchantment contributed far more to the poem's enormous popularity than did Charlemagne's triumph over his imperial rival, the pagan king Agramante, or
even than the eventual union of the disenchanted Ruggiero and the
heroic Bradamante from which the house of Ariosto's patrons, the
d'Este rulers of Ferrara, descends.

The *Odyssey*, the *Aeneid*, *Orlando furioso*, *Jerusalem Delivered*, and *The
Faerie Queene* all enjoyed great success in their own time and have continued to stand among the prime works of European literature. During the
long years of their composition, no less was expected of Petrarch's *Africa*
and Ronsard's *Franciade*, but neither was finished and neither has been
much read since its first publication. Yet taken together, particularly
when read in relation to their authors' other poetic writings, they pro-

vide an unusually telling example of the tensions characteristic of the new poetry, including Garcilaso's sonnet from Carthage. *Africa*, Petrarch's Latin account of the Roman general Scipio Africanus, and *The Franciade*, Ronsard's attempt to give France an *Aeneid*-like founding poem for a French empire, were intended to crown their respective author's careers, but were in fact overshadowed, as they have been overshadowed ever since, by their love sonnets, by Petrarch's vernacular *Rime sparse* and Ronsard's several books of *Amours*. The conflict between love and heroic action, a conflict that finds its place in each of their epic poems, as it does in every other epic in this tradition, is still more acutely represented in the poet's own amorous enthrallment, which draws him away from the imperial enterprise of heroic poetry. Though Petrarch insists in *Rime sparse* 186 that had Virgil and Homer seen Laura they too would have abandoned Aeneas, Achilles, and Ulysses to write of her and though he several times, as he does at the end of this sonnet, fuses the virtues of Laura and of Scipio, the prevailing sense is of a competition between the two and between the two poetic enterprises. Certainly in the opening sonnet of the sequence he writes of the present moment as an awakening from the folly that has long possessed him. And it is just such an awakening du Bellay tries to prompt in his friend Ronsard when he worries in his *Regrets* that Francus, the hero of Ronsard's *Franciade*, will never set sail for the destiny that awaits him and that we will "never see Ronsard except in love." As Dido trumps Aeneas, so Petrarch's Laura and Ronsard's Cassandre, Marie, and Hélène trump their authors' Scipio and Francus.

As for du Bellay, he did not himself attempt an epic. That job he left to Ronsard. But his *Regrets*, the sonnet sequence he wrote about the years he spent in Rome, is, among many other things, an autobiographical mock epic in which du Bellay himself takes on the role of Ulysses, Aeneas, and Ruggiero. And he, too, has his moment of Circean enchantment. In sonnets 87 through 90, he imagines that he, like the heroes of Homer, Virgil, and Ariosto, has fallen victim to a power capable of altering his very being and preventing his return to France, the enchanting power, in his case, of Italy itself. For the new poets of sixteenth-century Spain, Portugal, France, and England, and despite warnings like du Bellay's or the famous one issued to Englishmen by Roger Ascham in his *Schoolmaster*—*inglese italianato è un diavolo incarnato*—Italy was the ultimate seductress, a seductress to which their whole poetic enterprise depended on their succumbing. Du Bellay writes, after all, in an Italianate form, the sonnet sequence, and Ascham is promoting Italian humanist learning. Without undergoing a fundamental metamorphosis, the new poetry and the new learning would be inconceivable. In that sense, the interludes of erotic enchantment and metamorphosis are not a diversion from new poetic accomplishment. They are essential to it.

And, as it happens, there is at least one sixteenth-century epic that acknowledges the connection. Rather than making his Isle of Love a distraction from Vasco da Gama's heroic voyage to India, the subject of his *Lusiads,* Camões makes it a reward. Nor does he hide the intertextual relation between his orgiastic scene of triumphant debauchery and more familiar episodes of the sort we have been surveying. Venus, we are told, employs the same device on behalf of da Gama she "had once invoked to secure for Aeneas, her own son by Anchises, a friendly reception in Carthage," where Dido ruled. She bends, that is, the unknowingly awaiting queen's thoughts to love of her heroic protégé. But instead of a tragic outcome, Camões's Tethys, after satisfying da Gama's sensual desires, lifts him up to a summit of prophetic revelation and shows him the next ninety years of Portuguese accomplishment in Africa, India, and the Far East, a passage John Milton would later imitate in *Paradise Lost,* where he has the archangel Michael reveal to Adam the consequences of the Fall down to the coming of Christ and beyond to the last days. That scenes of Circean enchantment should evolve from culpable distraction to historical prophecy and then to divine revelation may seem little more than the playful whirligig of literary transmutation, a high-culture version of a trivial parlor game. But I suspect something deeper is going on. After all, as far back as the *Odyssey,* it is Circe who tells Odysseus that his way home must pass through Pluto's dark underworld, and even in the *Rime sparse* Petrarch's epiphanic vision of Laura, "her golden hair loosed to the breeze," echoes Aeneas's encounter with Venus on the Carthaginian shore in a way that transforms the poet's errant love into an epic quest, one whose political aim receives passionate expression thirty-eight poems later in the canzone "Italia mia." Erotic self-abandonment and imperial self-realization may not always be as much at odds with each other as one might suppose. On the contrary, one may lead to the other. And, at the very least, the poem or the poetic corpus that wholly neglects love in favor of empire will, by the standards of this extended fellowship, be sorely incomplete.

The oddest confirmation of the coupling of Circean enchantment and imperial longing comes near the end of the sixteenth century from the martyred magus Giordano Bruno. In one of the many extraordinarily bizarre twists that mark Bruno's hermetic thought, Circe, the very figure of forgetfulness, is granted a central position in his elaborately multilayered art of memory. Given the ancient recognition of the muses as the daughters of Memory and given the new poetry's obsessive insistence on its role as the prime guarantor of imperial recollection (an insistence perhaps most familiarly associated with the story that descends from Cicero to Petrarch, Castiglione, du Bellay, Camões, Spenser, and many others of Alexander's envious visit to the tomb of Achilles), to link Circe and memory can only seem a flagrant betrayal of all that the new poetry in its official, monumental guise strives for. What can a metamorphosed beast contribute to the storehouse of imperial memory? If, as du Bellay puts it, Rome's writings have kept the specter of Rome wandering the world long beyond empire's effective demise, what part can the Circean mistress of oblivion, the mistress of the very undoing to which Garcilaso's sonnet from Carthage inexorably leads, contribute to such a process? Yet, unlikely as his choice would appear, Bruno does elect Circe as the presiding deity of not one but two of his major memory treatises—his *Song of Circe* and his *Book of Seals*—and he gives her a large part in the one work he produced in the vein of the new poetry, his *Heroic Frenzies—Gli eroici furori.*

Dedicated to Sir Philip Sidney, the *Heroic Frenzies* begins with a violent diatribe against the female object of desire—"that eclipsed sun, that scourge, that disgust, that sink, that tomb, that latrine, that menstrum, that carrion, that quartan ague, that excessive injury and distortion of nature, which with surface appearance, a shadow, a phantom, a dream, a Circean enchantment put to the service of generation deceives us as a species of beauty"—particularly as she figures as the subject of Petrarchan poetry. In fact, Petrarch himself, whom Bruno considers little short of being "a madman fit to be chained," comes in for a considerable dose of unrestrained abuse. Even by Bruno's standards, this may seem an excessively odd stance to assume in a book addressed to a writer who himself came to be known as the English Petrarch. Could Bruno possibly have realized what he was doing? Perhaps he did. In both *Astrophil and Stella* and, even more, in the *Arcadia*, an epic-romance where one of Sidney's heroic princes turns shepherd for love and the other turns Amazon, Sidney confronts in the most acutely personal way the metamorphosing conflict between service to the state and erotic desire. And Bruno ends by providing a way out of this dilemma worthy of Camões, for he makes Circean enchantment and the oblivion it involves a necessary step on the way to a higher enlightenment he associates specifically with England. Recalling Virgil's characterization of the British as *penitus toto divisos orbe*—"cut off from the whole world"—he insists that English women and especially England's queen are divine creatures unlike mere mortal women, and he grants Elizabeth a culminating role as Circe's successor in the process of enlightenment. Circe can do no more than present the seals behind which the secrets of higher knowledge are hidden; "alone among all others," Elizabeth/Diana has the power to open them. Nor are ideas of universal empire further from

Bruno's thought than they are from the thought of any of the new poets we have been regarding. As he says in his *Ash Wednesday Supper*,

Of Elizabeth I speak, who by her title and royal dignity is inferior to no other monarch in the world; who for her wisdom and skill in sound government is second to none who hold the scepter. . . . If her earthly territory were a true reflection of the width and grandeur of her spirit, this great Amphitrite would bring far horizons within her girdle and enlarge the circumference of her dominion to include not only Britain and Ireland but some new world, as vast as the universal frame, where her all-powerful hand should have full scope to raise a united monarchy.

Could an Englishman, even one as imperially ambitious as Sidney, have hoped for more? Sidney's Elizabeth may have been a pusillanimous shirker—he hints at no less in the *Arcadia*—but neither he nor his fellow new poet, Edmund Spenser, who had his own doubts about the actual, as opposed to the ideally imagined, monarch of England, would have balked at the prospect of England's unworldly dominion being made to coincide with that of the universal frame of this terrestrial globe. If Circean self-abandonment leads to such a vision, its opposition to empire may be more apparent than real.

I began this chapter by rehearsing expectations so devoid of nuance and so commonplace that they could have been plucked from any country of western Europe. Language belongs in the company of empire, and empire is now being reborn. If language is to fulfill its destined role, as it must if empire is to live on in memory, it must be freed from vulgar oblivion and be given the artful and lasting finish of Greek and Latin. This was the task of the new poetry, a task accomplished first with Latin itself by Virgil and his fellow Augustan poets, then fourteen hundred years later by Petrarch with both a renewed Latin and a Latinized Tuscan vernacular, and finally in the sixteenth century by Bembo, Ariosto, Boscán, Garcilaso, du Bellay, Ronsard, Camões, Sidney, and Spenser with Latin, Italian, Spanish, French, Portuguese, and English. Extraordinarily difficult and even self-alienating in the execution—familiar languages were, after all, being made foreign—this process nevertheless took on its own familiarity and could be hailed, as Medina and Herrera hail Garcilaso, with little attention to what the poems actually say. But new-poetic alienation goes well beyond form. In passages where amorous enchantment opposes empire or recasts empire in terms more consonant with poetry's own self-immolating identity than with the triumphal, all-dominating identity of empire, poetry asserts a role, self-destructive as it may appear, that makes its own claim on at least an invisible transcendence.

When Virgil willed the *Aeneid* to the flames, could he have forgotten the fate of Dido? Or was he rather, in those final moments, identifying with her? Along with the story of Alexander's envy of Achilles for having found a Homer to broadcast his deeds, Augustus's intervention, exercising his imperial prerogative to break the poet's will and save his poem, was the Renaissance's favorite story of the ideal relation of poetry and empire. But such happy accord is not what the poets, as opposed to their canonizing commentators, claimed most often to have experienced. Petrarch never found his ideal Scipio in life, and he left unfinished and unpublished in favor of his vernacular rhymes the poem meant to set forth the pattern of such a ruler. Similarly favoring his erotic verse, Ronsard abandoned his epic at a still earlier stage in its composition. Du Bellay returned to France only to discover that the French court was no more hospitable to poetic truth than the papal court in Rome had been. Camões and Spenser end their great poems despairing of the recognition their art would deserve. "And now, my Muse," sings Camões, "let there be an end; for my lyre is no longer in tune and my voice grows hoarse, not from my song, but from seeing that those to whom I sing are become hard of hearing and hard of heart," while for Spenser the Blatant Beast of envy and detraction is once more loosed upon the world, "Ne may this homely verse, of many meanest, / Hope to escape his venemous despite." Fearing such despite, Tasso stripped the romance from his *Jerusalem Delivered*, transforming it into the chastely unreadable *Jerusalem Conquered*, and Sidney did something almost as bad in rewriting the often comic *Old Arcadia* into the relentlessly high-minded *New*. And not even that was enough for Sidney. Like Virgil, he ended by demanding that his work be burned, for, as he was reported to have said on his deathbed, "he then discovered, not only the imperfection, but the vanity of these shadows, how daintily soever limned, and [saw] that even beauty itself, in all earthly complexions, was more apt to allure men to evil than to frame any goodness in them." And Ariosto, in what must be among the most extraordinary examples of imperial doublethink, worked simultaneously for well over a decade not only on his victorious and public *Furioso* but also on five private and unpublished cantos—*I cinque canti*—that systematically undo the very accomplishments he had been so eager to celebrate in the poem to which those cantos would be appended. As David Quint has so perceptively put it, Ariosto wrote a *Pharsalia*, an epic of imperial loss, to complete and reverse his *Aeneid*, his epic of imperial triumph.

Is the new poetry the companion of empire? That certainly is its most obvious undertaking. But, as we have seen, from Virgil through Petrarch and on to the poets of the sixteenth century, that companionship is always strained, always at least partially thwarted, always shadowed by other commitments. And nowhere is that more complexly, more variously, or more movingly true than in Garcilaso's sonnet from Carthage, a poem that marvelously combines in its brief length imperial ambition, self-conscious poetic aspiration, and Dido-like self-immolation—all forces we can see working through the new poetry as a whole—with two further widely shared engagements that I have not so far explored, a commitment to place and a commitment to male friendship. It is thus to Garcilaso's poem that we should now turn.

2.

Las armas y el furor de Marte / Arms and the fury of Mars

> . . . *las armas y el furor de Marte,*
> *que con su propria fuerça el africano*
> *suelo regando, hazen que el romano*
> *imperio reverdezca en esta parte . . .*

[. . . arms and the fury of Mars, which, watering the African soil with its own strength, make the Roman Empire flourish once again in this region . . .]

Arma virumque. So familiar were these opening words of the *Aeneid*— "Arms and the man"—to sixteenth-century readers, or at least to readers who had anything of a humanist education, that even a small change would be immediately recognized as significant. Camões made just such a change in *The Lusiads.* He began *As armas e os barões*, thus proposing to sing not "arms and the man" but rather "arms and the men." Despite the central role Camões gives Vasco da Gama, the Portuguese nation, and especially its *barões*, its "noblemen" or "barons," are to be his subject. In the miniature epic that is his sonnet from Carthage, Garcilaso's alteration of the Virgilian opening is no less significant. Recognizing no individual hero nor even any particular nation, he sings "arms and the fury of Mars."

That Garcilaso should begin with large impersonal forces, arms and the fury of the god of war, makes sense. Charles V's North African triumph took its place in a long and astounding string of victories that may be thought to have begun in 1520 with the one that would in all likelihood have remained most intimately bound up with Garcilaso's consciousness, the defeat of his brother Pedro Laso and his fellow Castilian rebels in the revolt of the *comuneros*, and that continued beyond Tunis and beyond even Garcilaso's own death to the battle of Mühlberg in 1547, where Charles and his imperial forces overcame the Lutheran princes and took captive their leader John Frederick of Saxony. In between came Cortés's conquest of Tenochtitlán and the Aztec empire of Mexico in 1521, the battle of Pavia and the capture of Charles's greatest European rival, the French king Francis I, in 1525, the sack of Rome and the captivity of Pope Clement VII in 1527, the successful response to Suleiman the Magnificent outside Vienna in 1532, and Pizarro's conquest of Atahualpa's Inca empire also in 1532. Clearly, something beyond personal or even national prowess, something beyond the most astute imperial strategy, is needed to explain such victories. To have overcome in a little over a quarter century a major popular uprising, the two largest and most powerful New World empires, the greatest figures of European politics, a king, a pope, and a band of German princes, in addition to the Turkish sultan and his Moorish surrogate suggests the workings of forces well beyond our normal ken, something like the sheer power of arms and the fury of Mars.

If events of this magnitude cried out for interpretation, no such event lent itself more readily to interpretive framing than the conquest to which Garcilaso's poem is devoted, the conquest of Tunis. Still hailed today by historians such as James Tracey and Geoffrey Parker as Charles V's "greatest military triumph," the Tunis expedition brings together more of what we have seen working through the epic tradition than any other. The very ground on which it was fought was sacred to both Virgil's *Aeneid* and Petrarch's *Africa,* while the encounter of pagan and Christian reminds us of *Orlando furioso, Jerusalem Delivered, The Lusiads,* and *The Faerie Queene,* a poem that freely transforms the king of Spain into the sultan just to fit the familiar pattern. Yet neat as the fit between the Tunis expedition and the epic tradition may appear, there were in fact notably different emphases, differences in which Garcilaso's sonnet took an active part.

To get an initial idea of how interpretation most commonly turned, here is what the Italian humanist Paolo Giovio wrote to Charles himself in a letter that accompanied Giovio's own account of the battle: "Your Majesty's glorious and incomparable victory of Tunis seems to me, for the respect of the Christian faith, most worthy above the others of eternal fame." Giovio's qualification—"for the respect of the Christian faith"—points toward an interpretive frame that dominated the sixteenth-century understanding of what Charles had accomplished, a frame that is conspicuously absent from Garcilaso's poem. By this reckoning, the conquest of Tunis was a chivalric crusade waged in the name of Christendom against the infidel Moors and Turks. As is commonly the case in such matters, the reality was considerably more complicated. Not only was the victory less complete and less lasting than imperial propagandists were inclined to acknowledge, but the opposing sides were also less clearly distinguishable and the mode of warfare less obviously chivalric. And still more striking for our purposes, another interpretive frame competed for representational preeminence. Instead of marking a modern renewal of medieval crusading, the conquest of Tunis recalled the ancient destruction of nearby Carthage and marked the rebirth of triumphant and all-governing Rome.

However large a part such framings played in the minds of the participants themselves, the first incitement to action came from elsewhere. For years the Berber corsair Kheir-ed-Din—better known in Europe as Barbarossa—had disrupted shipping and raided coastal communities in the western Mediterranean from his base in Algiers. In 1534 the sultan Suleiman the Magnificent, who just two years earlier had, as we have noticed, threatened the Habsburg stronghold of Vienna, named Barbarossa admiral of the Turkish fleet. Emboldened by this new dignity and the forces that went with it, Barbarossa immediately attacked the coast of southern Italy, another of the many parts of Europe under Charles's rule, and seized the strategically proximate port of Tunis, overthrowing its ruler, Mulay Hasan, who had been a vassal of the Spanish crown since the time of Charles's maternal grandfather, King Ferdinand of Aragon. And what made the situation still more dangerous was that the emperor's chief European rival, the French king Francis I, was backing Suleiman and Barbarossa with money and arms. Clearly Charles had to act.

From his Portuguese and papal allies and from his own vast European empire, he summoned an armada that when finally assembled included some four hundred ships and nearly thirty thousand men, paid for in large part by the Inca treasure of Atahualpa, which just months before had fortuitously reached the emperor's Spanish coffers. This huge fleet, the largest ever seen in Charles's long reign, set sail from Sardinia on June 14, 1535, and disembarked two days later on the African coast near the site of ancient Carthage. Rather than attacking Tunis directly, Charles laid siege to the outlying fortress of Goleta. After nearly a month of sometimes deadly sorties and skirmishes, including one on June 22 in which Garcilaso was injured in the mouth and the right arm, Goleta fell to the imperial troops. Charles then marched on Tunis, which was easily taken thanks to an uprising of thousands of Christian slaves who had captured the armory and overrun the citadel. Though the people of Tunis surrendered with no further resistance, Charles rewarded his unruly troops by allowing them to sack the city, something they did with a fervor that recalled the notorious sack of Rome eight years earlier. Charles then reinstalled the brutal Mulay Hasan as the ruler of Tunis and on August 17 set sail for Sicily, after a stay in North Africa of barely two months.

What did this unquestionable victory really accomplish? Considerably less than might have been hoped. Though Charles succeeded in destroying much of Barbarossa's fleet and recapturing Tunis, his plan to follow up with an attack on Algiers was frustrated by adverse winds. As for Barbarossa, he slipped away before the fall of Tunis and was soon harassing Minorca and the coast of Spain. And when in 1541 Charles equipped a second armada with the intention of taking Algiers and completing the job left half done six years earlier, his fleet was wrecked in a storm without ever reaching its target. But nowhere is the long-term futility of the Tunis expedition more painfully suggested than in the next notable appearance of the fortress of Goleta in Spanish literature. In part 1 of *Don Quixote,* the tale told by a Spanish captain who had recently escaped captivity in Algiers includes an account of the fall of Goleta to the Turks in 1574. Instead of lamenting the loss, the captain, whose experiences and opinions nearly match those of Cervantes himself, gives thanks for it. "To many it seemed, as it seemed to me," he says, "that heaven bestowed on Spain a special grace and mercy in allowing the destruction of that storehouse and refuge of wickedness, that gulf or sponge and sinkhole where without profit infinite sums of money are wasted with no other purpose than to preserve the memory of its having been happily won by the invincible Charles V, as though to make his memory eternal, as it is and will always be, those stones were needed." Less than forty years after its capture, Goleta had become an expensive and otherwise useless monument to the memory of Charles V.

But almost from the first the North African expedition functioned more as a monument than as a strategically decisive military accomplishment. Barbarossa's actions did demand a response. Ensconced in Tunis and allied with Suleiman the Magnificent and Francis I, he posed a threat Charles could not ignore. For purely practical reasons, Charles needed to dislodge him and retake Tunis. But Charles, his advisers, and many other supporters with agendas of their own also recognized this as an opportunity to make a statement about the very nature of his imperial rule, and they made sure that their various statements would reach as large an audience as possible. Though the emperor may not have known that among his Spanish officers was a poet capable of giving lasting expression to the events in which they were both participating, he did make other, more obvious arrangements to guarantee that what he was doing in North Africa would not go unnoticed. Besides writing his own account in a series of letters sent from the battlefield, he employed others to broadcast his triumph in a variety of ways. The emperor's secretary, Antoine Perrenin, wrote an account in French, which was later translated and published in Latin, and still other eyewitness accounts came from Luis Ávila y Zúñiga and Martín García Cerezeda and were then used as the basis for more elaborate renditions, Ávila's by Juan

Ginés de Sepúlveda, to whom it was delivered by Garcilaso himself, and Cerezeda's by Alonso de Santa Cruz. In addition the emperor met personally with Paolo Giovio immediately on his return to Italy and supplied him with information for the history Giovio planned to write.

Nor were other media neglected. The renowned neo-Latin poet Johannes Secundus, another of the emperor's secretaries, was commissioned to produce an epic poem on the Tunis expedition, a project left unrealized at the poet's early death. In the meantime, a host of writers, artists, and craftsmen were set to work on the series of triumphal entries that greeted the emperor as he made his way over the next several months through the Italian peninsula from Palermo, to Messina, Naples, Rome, Siena, Florence, and Lucca. Never before had Italy seen such an "explosion," as Roy Strong has aptly called it, "of symbolic pageantry." And there were a number of more lasting tributes as well: Medals and statues, paintings, poems, and engravings, a series of frescoes in the imperial palace in Granada and the most grandiose collection of tapestries that had ever been devoted to a contemporary event. Based on drawings made during the campaign itself by the court artist Jan Cornelisz Vermeyen, who was brought along precisely for that purpose, these twelve enormous tapestries, with their detailed moment-by-moment representation of the Tunis expedition, from the mustering of the troops in Barcelona to the final departure from North Africa, served as a regular backdrop at Habsburg dynastic events for generations to come. (They made a first appearance in London in 1554 for the wedding of Charles's son Philip to Queen Mary Tudor.) Long before its loss to the Turks in 1574, the defensive emplacement Charles left in Goleta to secure his African conquest may, as Cervantes suggested, have become a useless sinkhole of men and resources, but the memory of Charles's glorious victory there remained a defining feature of Habsburg self-understanding well into the reigns of his son and even his grandson.

Memory is specifically evoked by Garcilaso's sonnet, but not memory of the event in which the poet was taking part. That was still too close. Instead the emperor's African victory brings something else to remembrance. It recalls "the art and ancient Italian valor by whose strength and valorous hand Africa was leveled from end to end"—recalls, that is, the ancient Punic Wars of Rome, recalls the triumphs of Scipio Africanus and his younger namesake, recalls the destruction of Carthage. And more than just a memory, this is, as Garcilaso presents it, a restoration. Through Charles's actions, through "arms and the fury of Mars," the Roman Empire has once again been made to flourish in North Africa and, by extension, through the whole extent of the far-flung Habsburg lands, including lands that Rome itself had never ruled.

But this historical recollection, powerfully compelling as it is, needs to be read in relation to another, to the remembrance suggested by Paolo Giovio's "for respect of the Christian faith." From its inception, the Tunis expedition came cloaked, as I have already suggested, in memories of the crusades. Peter Burke has neatly summarized the most salient evidence: "The conquest of Tunis . . . was officially declared to be a crusade by Pope Paul III. It was also presented as such from the moment of Charles's pilgrimage to the shrine of the Virgin Mary at Montserrat in Calabria before he sailed for Africa. The interpretation was confirmed by Charles's remark that 'the crucified Savior shall be our captain.'"

It is easy to see why Charles and his advisers would have wanted to remember the crusades. Turning the attack on Barbarossa into a religious war effectively neutralized Francis I, who risked being cast as the enemy of Christendom if he continued to support the infidel, and it made even Charles's German Protestant subjects eager to send troops. And perhaps no less important, it fit Charles's own idea of himself as the destined champion of the Christian faith. A chivalric and crusading ethos had a large place in the Burgundian court where Charles was raised, especially in association with the Order of the Golden Fleece, whose head he became in 1516. And from his Austrian imperial forebears, his grandfather Maximilian I and his great-grandfather Frederick III, he inherited millenarian ideas of a universal theocratic empire. Given the vast and unprecedented extent of his holdings, including not only more of the Old World than had been ruled by any one man since Charlemagne but also a New World unknown prior to the sixteenth century, he might reasonably imagine himself to be the long-awaited "Last World Emperor," who would unite the whole globe as "one flock" under "one shepherd." A destiny of that sort was, in fact, what his chancellor, Mercurio Gattinara, told him to expect. "Sire," wrote Gattinara after Charles's election as emperor, "God has been very merciful to you: he has raised you above all the kings and princes of Christendom to a power such as no sovereign has enjoyed since your ancestor Charles the Great. He has set you on the way towards a world monarchy, towards the uniting of all Christendom under a single shepherd." And just a few years before the Tunis expedition, this expectation was echoed by Ariosto in the fifteenth canto of *Orlando furioso*, where, from the vantage of Charlemagne's reign, a figure of wisdom is made to prophesy the coming of an emperor of Austrian and of Spanish blood under whose rule God intends there to be "only one flock, only one shepherd." When Charles mustered his troops, as the Vermeyen tapestries show him to have done, under the banner of the Apocalyptic Woman, the woman described in Revelation 12 as clothed in the sun with the moon at her feet, such prophecies could well have been thought on their way to accomplishment, and the planned attack on Tunis could easily have been understood, as both the pope and the emperor invited their followers to understand it, as a crucial battle in a holy crusade—perhaps even the ultimate crusade.

But that is not the understanding Garcilaso's sonnet presents. Though it seems likely that Garcilaso had the 1532 edition of Ariosto with him on the Tunis campaign—two phrases in the sonnet come from *Orlando furioso* and there are other borrowings in the elegy written to Boscán a few weeks later—he does not share Ariosto's apocalyptic vision of Charles's imperial destiny, nor does he give any attention to the clash of Christian and infidel in the Tunis expedition. Indeed, nowhere in the six poems he wrote during these months do religious differences or the sense of a religious mission come to the surface, with the single exception of the opening stanzas of his Latin ode to Juan Ginés de Sepúlveda, which allude to "the bow of religion" and the "pious king." But these, he says, are to be the subjects of Sepúlveda's muse, as he writes the history with which he has been charged. They are not Garcilaso's subjects. Instead he avoids all mention of religion and wholly neglects the king's piety, even when, as in the elegy to the duke of Alba, those topics would seem to be precisely suited to his rhetorical needs. How in a poem like this one, where he is consoling his friend and patron on the death of Alba's younger brother, Don Bernardino, can he say nothing of the sacred cause for which Bernardino had fought? And yet not only does he say nothing. He ardently denies that there is anything to say. What, he asks, is won by the horrors of war? "Some glory? Some prizes or gratitude? He who reads our story will know: it will be clear that like dust in the wind, so will our arduous endeavor dissolve before whomever attempts to uphold it."

Not all Garcilaso's poems that arose from the Tunis expedition are this unremittingly bleak. Like the sonnet from Carthage, the elegy addressed to Boscán begins with a more positive remembrance of the glory of Rome. Here Garcilaso calls Charles "Caesar Africanus," thus making explicit the identification with Scipio Africanus that the sonnet only suggests. And he also recalls the "good Trojan" Anchises, the father of Aeneas, whose ashes are buried in that part of Sicily from where he is writing. But he again neglects the religious confrontation that made Charles and his advisers present the Tunis expedition as a crusade. The question appears inevitable: Why this neglect? Why, when he is not dismissing altogether the military accomplishment of the campaign in which he has just participated (an issue to which I will return), does Garcilaso insist on a Roman interpretation? Why does he ask us to see Charles as a new Scipio and his North African victory as a rebirth of the Roman Empire?

Connections between Charles's imperial office and ancient Rome were nothing new. Charles was, after all, the Holy *Roman* Emperor, a title that found its justification in a centuries-old theory of *translatio imperii* according to which the empire of Rome had been transferred to the Germanic North. And beginning in 1529, when Charles first traveled to Italy to be crowned by the pope in Bologna, a self-consciously Roman style, a style *all'antica*, overtook the court and the emperor himself. On the advice of his chancellor Gattinara, the long-haired, clean-shaven Burgundian prince who appears in every painting, medal, statue, and engraving made prior to the Italian trip, "recreated himself," in the words of Wim Blockmans, "as the incarnation of a Roman emperor." Not even the association with Scipio was new. On the occasion of the imperial coronation, the town gate of Bologna was decorated with an equestrian statue of Scipio along with medallions of Caesar, Augustus, Vespasian, and Trajan. And in the triumphal progress through Italy that followed the Tunis expedition, Scipio, whether the elder or the younger or an indistinct melding of the two, was everywhere. In Medina, a classical column topped with a marble bust of Scipio greeted the emperor with the motto, "Charles, you will be divine, you will be Africanus"; another bust of Scipio marked his entry into Naples; and in Rome enormous paintings of the African triumphs of the first and second Scipio and of Charles himself proclaimed him to be the "third Africanus." Nor were such identifications confined to the immediate aftermath of the Tunis expedition. Six years later, at the emperor's lavish entry into Milan, he was still being called the "new Scipio."

What most powerfully links Garcilaso's poems, including most obviously the sonnet from Carthage, to these Italian festivals is not only the emphasis both put on classical Roman recollections, including memories of the two Scipios, but also their neglect of the chivalric remembrances that for Charles himself and for many of those who accompanied him were at least as important. In the Italian entries, as Roy Strong has remarked, "Charles is always the Roman Emperor, crowned with laurel, his victories celebrated as emulating those recorded by Livy. . . . Unlike the North there were no allusions to knightly chivalry, only to the *imperator;* the victories were of valiant Romans over Carthaginians, not of invading knights over infidel Turks." This similarity both in emphasis and in neglect suggests a first answer to our question about the way in which Garcilaso chose to represent Charles's Tunis expedition. Garcilaso's vision of those events is essentially Italian. To a greater extent than even the emperor himself, Garcilaso had been remade by his contact with Italy and with the humanist culture that was flourishing there. For Charles, classical ideas of empire merely complemented the northern chivalric and millenarian ideas with which he had been raised. He could be both a crusading knight and a new Scipio. That one pose suggested a deep continuity with his medieval forebears while the other suggested rather a radical disavowal of that medieval past seemed not to bother him. But for the Italians who scripted and designed his post-Tunis progress of 1535 and 1536, such syncretism—a syncretism that still reigned in Ariosto's *Orlando furioso*—had little appeal. In a divided and defeated Italy that during the previous four decades had been repeatedly ravaged by the contending forces of Germany, Spain, and France, the opportunity to claim the emperor as a Roman and to hail his North African victory as the return of a time when Italy was the political and military center of the known world was too good to pass up.

But why would this Italian view have so captured the imagination of a Spaniard like Garcilaso? Nothing in his work suggests that he shared the political ambition of the Italians. Nor does it seem likely that he would. At a time when Italy's sufferings were more than matched by Spain's growing ascendancy, there can have been few Spaniards who longed to see Rome restored *in* Rome, a city the imperial troops had sacked in 1527. But the steps leading to that ascendancy—the union of Aragon and Castile, the conquest of Granada, the discovery, conquest, and settlement of the New World, the election of Spain's king as Holy Roman Emperor, the defeat of the French, the spread of Spanish and imperial power in Italy—did prompt at least a few Spaniards to imagine that Rome might be restored in Spain, that just as Charles was declared the new Scipio, so Spain might emerge as the new Rome. Whether Garcilaso was one of these is impossible to say. But what remains unmistakable is that he was bent, for whatever reason, on producing in Spanish an Italian and Roman poetic art, an ambition that both gained in clarity and achieved remarkable fruition in just the years that included the Tunis expedition. Thus when in his sonnet from Carthage Garcilaso celebrates the rebirth of the Roman Empire and hails the return to memory of an ancient Italian art, he is talking at least as much about his own poem as he is about his sovereign's victory. The large impersonal forces with which he begins thus turn out to have a quite personal application. The new Scipio, who implicitly gives body to "arms and the fury of Mars," calls forth in the person of Garcilaso himself a new Virgil and a new Petrarch.

3.
El arte italïano / Italian art

han reduzido a la memoria el arte
y el antiguo valor italïano,
por cuya fuerça y valerosa mano
Africa se aterró de parte a parte.

[have led back to memory the art and ancient Italian valor by whose strength and valorous hand Africa was leveled from end to end.]

The project of reforming Spanish poetry along Italian lines was born in the precincts of empire. As Boscán tells the story in the famous letter to the duchess of Soma that introduces the second book of his and Garcilaso's collected works, it was in Granada in 1526, shortly following the emperor's marriage to Isabel of Portugal, that the Venetian ambassador, Andrea Navagero, who was also a renowned humanist and poet, suggested that Boscán try writing Spanish poems in Italian meters. No firm evidence assures us that Garcilaso accompanied the court from Seville, where the imperial marriage had been solemnized, to Granada, but whether he was there or not, he soon joined his friend in following Navagero's advice. Like Boscán, he abandoned the eight-syllable line that had long dominated Spanish verse, including the poems he and Boscán had written up to this time, and adopted the eleven-syllable line made most familiar by Petrarch and his sixteenth-century Italian followers. And with the change in the metrical line came a no less decisive change in generic form. For *coplas* and other traditional Spanish genres, they substituted sonnets and *canciones,* the very forms Petrarch used for his vernacular poems.

So abrupt and so sweeping a change—in effect, the rejection of a native poetic identity in favor of a foreign one—was bound to provoke opposition, and so it did. As soon as he set to work, Boscán reports, he encountered a host of objections. The new verses violated established taste; they spread their rhymes too sparsely; they seemed more like prose than verse; they were good only for women. But the most telling rebuke came years later, after the doubly posthumous publication of the

Works of Boscán and Some by Garcilaso de la Vega, when Cristóbal de Castillejo mockingly called on the Holy Inquisition to investigate "this newly formed sect . . . in Spain as strange and new as Luther's in Germany." Boscán, Garcilaso, and their followers "can rightly be punished," Castillejo continues, "as if they were Anabaptists, since they are getting rebaptized according to their own laws, and they call themselves Petrarchists. They have rejected the faith in Castilian meters, and they lose their souls seeking after Italian ones." Then, in an amusing Italianate sonnet of his own, Castillejo imagines Boscán and Garcilaso in the afterlife meeting up with their Spanish troubadour predecessors. At first the two groups eye one another with suspicion and hostility. Then they recognize by their clothes that both are "gentle Spanish knights." But when the troubadours hear Garcilaso and Boscán speak in "a new language, mixed with foreign poetry," they gaze at them with wonder as though they were foreigners (*con ojos los miraban de estranjeros*).

But, as others, like Herrera and Medina, were quick to assert, such strangeness was just what Spanish needed. Herrera talks of Garcilaso's having opened "the way for those who will follow so that Spanish poetry will not be lost in the obscurity of ignorance," while Medina associates that obscurity with former subjection. We must, he says, "throw from our necks the yoke with which the barbarians have oppressed Spain and . . . recover the liberty of our fatherland." Neither Boscán nor Garcilaso goes quite so far. Neither asks that we consider traditional Spanish verse a mark of ignorance and subjection. But Boscán does insist that the new Italianate forms are "more serious," "more artful," and "much better," while Garcilaso, in the prefatory letter he wrote to Boscán's translation of Castiglione's *Book of the Courtier,* laments the lack of good writing in Spanish. "I do not know what plagues us that hardly anyone has written anything in our tongue except what we could easily have done without." That both should have felt the need to see Castiglione's book translated into Spanish is one indication of their cultural estrangement. Their project to reform Spanish verse is another. Through their identification with the imperial court, they had moved into a space from which the traditional culture of Spain, both its courtly culture and its literary culture, could only appear inadequate, even barbarous.

Writing in Spanish—that is, in Castilian—rather than in the Catalan of his native Barcelona was for Boscán already an act on self-estrangement. Garcilaso's estrangement was more subtle, but no less profound. When in the poem that always appears as the first of his sonnets, he echoes Petrarch's retrospective wonder at the distance he has traveled— *Quando me paro a contemplar mi 'stado / y a ver los passos por dó m'han traýdo* . . . (When I pause to consider my state and to look back on the steps that have led me here . . .)—he might just as well be talking about cultural dislocation as about love. Petrarchan self-alienation provided a particularly apt figure for the cultural self-alienation that prompted the new poetry all over Europe. And in Garcilaso's case, as in Petrarch's own, there is, as we have seen, much to explain why he might have felt estranged. First called to court when he was not yet twenty, involved almost immediately in military action against the *comuneros* party of his brother and his neighbors, thrown into the company of people like Boscán, Navagero, and even Castiglione himself, exiled from Spain, stationed at the viceregal court in Naples, introduced into the leading literary circles of southern Italy, including the Accademia Pontaniana, in whose meetings he took an active part, Garcilaso had, indeed, traveled a long road. Though he still wrote in Spanish, he had been culturally transformed, and so, too, had his poetry.

His sonnet from Carthage marks a crucial step in that transformation. Unlike Boscán and the leading new poets of France and England, Garcilaso wrote no literary manifesto. But this sonnet, with its declaration of the rebirth of Rome and of the Italian art that made Rome immortal, comes as close as anything he did write to defining a literary program. Not that the ostensible subject of the poem is poetry. It isn't. Arms and the fury of Mars have restored imperial rule and have brought back to memory the ancient Italian art of warfare. But this classicizing interpretation of the emperor's North African victory is shaped to accommodate Garcilaso's own poetic ambition. If the Roman Empire was being reborn, could an imperial poetry, a poetry written in the language of the emperor's largest and most powerful kingdom, be far behind?

The emphasis on Rome had a still more particular relevance to the turn Garcilaso's work was taking at just this time. In his letter to the duchess of Soma, Boscán says that the Italian hendecasyllabics he and Garcilaso were imitating descend ultimately from Greek and Latin verse and are suitable for any kind of poem found among the best authors of antiquity, but the only genres he specifically recommends are the more modern, Petrarchan ones, the sonnet and the *canción*. In the years between Boscán's meeting with Navagero and Garcilaso's exile from Spain, these would also appear to have been the only genres the two friends attempted. Thus though they were energetically Italianizing Spanish poetry, they had not yet Romanized it. That changed, at least for Garcilaso, with his move to Italy. Inspired by the Neapolitan humanist community that he was now frequenting and especially by his contact in Naples and elsewhere with such figures as Pietro Bembo, Bernardo Tasso, Mario Galeota, Scipione Capece, Antonio Telesio, and Girolamo Seripando, he began adopting classical models. In addition to the blank-verse Horatian epistle, the two elegies, and the Latin ode to Sepúlveda, all of which he wrote during the months he was involved in the Tunis campaign and its immediate aftermath, these last years of his life saw the production of his three eclogues, his two other Latin odes, and a Horatian ode in Spanish, his "Ode ad florem Gnidi," poems for which, as for the others, there was no precedent in Spanish.

What I said earlier of the new poetry generally is no less true here. A break of this magnitude—now not only from the prior forms of Spanish verse, but also from the Petrarchan manner he and Boscán had been following—required justification. And in this case, Garcilaso's sonnet from Carthage makes that justification available. Like the Italian artists who had designed the emperor's coronation in Bologna—an event Garcilaso attended—and like those who would soon be mounting the triumphal entries that would mark the emperor's return from Tunis, Garcilaso casts Charles as a Roman general so as to provide the appropriate political setting for his own Roman art. Here the vaunted companionship of language and empire serves particularly the poet and provides a guide as to how his poems should be understood. And, indeed, if we look more closely not only at this poem but at all six of the poems Garcilaso wrote during the course of the Tunis expedition, what becomes quickly apparent is that poetic artfulness emerges to make a claim that is only nominally dependent on empire. Yes, Garcilaso is the emperor's soldier, the emperor's diplomat. But he is also a poet, and, as such, he has technical engagements—engagements of craft, one might say—that have little to do with his more obvious imperial duties. Craft alone does not identify him as a poet. Love has, if anything, a larger and more insistent part, one that, as we may anticipate from our look at Dido, Circe, and their sisters, pits poetry still more self-consciously against empire, and to love we will need eventually to turn. But for now let us see how in this moment of extraordinary creative ferment, a moment that had as its background one of the greatest military enterprises of Charles V's long career, Garcilaso reflected on and actively practiced his literary art.

The first of the six poems, the epistle to Boscán, is the one that says least about the great events swirling in the background. Indeed, it says nothing at all about them. But this is perhaps not surprising. Garcilaso was, after all, traveling on a confidential mission and was writing from potentially hostile territory. On August 15, 1534, within days of Barbarrosa's capture of Tunis, Garcilaso was sent from Naples to the emperor's court in Palencia with the latest news. On September 29, he left Palencia with the emperor's response and traveled overland, stopping, it is usually assumed, in Barcelona for a brief visit with Boscán, and then continuing in haste on his way to Naples across the south of France. His poem is dated from Avignon "where Petrarch's bright flame was born and where the ashes of this flame remain" on October 12. The allusion to Petrarch's Laura, whose burial place in Avignon had recently been identified and had become a site of pilgrimage, suggests the poem's self-consciously literary ambiance, but still more significant is the careful opening discussion of the "free and pure informality . . . far from affected weightiness" that belongs to a "learned epistle" (*culta epístola*). *Descuydo*, the word I have translated as "informality," was used by Boscán and Garcilaso in their translation of *The Book of the Courtier* for Castiglione's crucial notion of courtly *sprezzatura*, that aristocratic ability to perform at the highest level with no apparent effort. An Horatian epistle to a close friend, especially an epistle written in seemingly artless *versos sueltos*—that is, in unrhymed or blank verse—provides a perfect display of such *descuydo*. The moment is one of apparent liberty—"I allow freer and looser rein to my fancy than to my horse"—and the style accords itself to that liberty.

But this is, I need hardly say, a highly artful artlessness. Garcilaso may have made the values of Castiglione's *Courtier* his own, but he had also absorbed the values of his fellow humanists in Naples, particularly their keen interest in Horace. Never before had such an epistle been written in Spanish. Such things do not happen by accident. For all his apparent *descuydo*, Garcilaso defines a new genre for himself and for all future poets of his language. And he does so both with great deliberation and, though, given the nature of his embassy, this can only remain implicit, in tandem with his imperial duty. New poetry is here quite literally accompanying the work of empire. Garcilaso composes this, the first Horatian epistle in Spanish, as he carries a critical dispatch, orders on which the impending invasion of North Africa depend, from the emperor to Don Pedro de Toledo, the emperor's viceroy in Naples. Yet the poem itself, which concerns Garcilaso's feelings for Boscán and the deplorable conditions he finds on the roads of France, seems to have nothing to do with the great business of empire. Poetry accompanies empire only to ignore or disavow it.

Such disavowal becomes more nearly explicit in the elegy Garcilaso wrote Boscán from Trapani in southern Italy nearly a year later in August 1535, immediately following the successful conquest of Tunis. The poem begins with epic recollections—"Here, Boscán, where Mantuan Virgil preserves the good Trojan Anchises's ashes with eternal name and life"—and with a salute to the recent triumph of Charles V, whose identification with Scipio, only implied in the Carthage sonnet, is now made plain—"under the illustrious standard of Caesar Africanus, we find ourselves, the victors, gathered." But if we think this opening will lead to further celebration of that triumph, we are quickly disabused. Instead, Garcilaso devotes the next fifteen lines to a wry account of his fellow soldiers' generally unheroic motivations before catching himself up with a sudden sense of violated literary decorum: "But where has my pen taken

me? Step by step I slip into satire, and what I am writing you is an elegy."
And, as soon becomes clear, elegy is antithetical not only to satire but
also to the kind of heroic verse we might have expected to follow from
the introductory allusion to Charles V and the military events of the previous months. Such antipathy belongs to ancient poetic practice, where
it is associated particularly with Ovid and his anti-Virgilian aesthetic. But
here it is rooted in a more personal system of values that are only partially literary. For Garcilaso, military duties are one thing; poetry and its
pleasures are quite another.

A persistent sense of resentment and even repugnance toward the
military duties and accomplishments that were the very stuff of imperial
service runs through much of Garcilaso's later verse. We have already
encountered him in the elegy to the duke of Alba on the death of Alba's
brother quite astonishingly announcing that our "arduous endeavor"—
that is, the Tunis expedition itself—will dissolve "like dust in the wind."
Taken in its full context, the famous image in the third eclogue, written
perhaps a year later than the elegy to Boscán during what was to be for
Garcilaso the fatal Provence campaign, of the soldier-poet *tomando ora la
espada, ora la pluma* (taking up now the sword and now the pen) is no
more favorable to the sword. And the opening of the "Ode ad florem
Gnidi," which also belongs to the months or year immediately proximate to the Tunis expedition, sets up the opposition at length and
makes Garcilaso's preference unmistakable:

> *Si de mi baxa lira*
> *tanto pudiesse el son que en un momento*
> *aplacase la ira*
> *del animoso viento*
> *y la furia del mar y el movimiento,*
>
> *y en ásperas montañas*
> *con el süave canto enterneciesse*
> *las fieras alimañas,*
> *los árboles moviesse*
> *y al son confusamente los truxiesse:*
>
> *no pienses que cantado*
> *sería de mí, hermosa flor de Gñido,*
> *el fiero Marte ayrado,*
> *a muerte convertido,*
> *de polvo y sangre y sudor teñido,*

ni aquellos capitanes
en las sublimes ruedas colocados,
por quien los alemanes,
el fiero cuello atados,
y los franceses van domesticados;

mas solamente aquella
fuerça de tu beldad seria cantada.

[If from my lowly lyre the sound were so powerful that in a moment it would appease the anger of the raging wind and the fury of the sea and its movement, and in the rough mountains with gentle song it could touch wild beasts, move the trees and draw them confusedly after the sound, do not think that I would sing, beautiful flower of Gnido, of proud and wrathful Mars, given over to death, stained with dust and blood and sweat, nor of those captains mounted on sublime wheels by whom the proud necks of the Germans are bound and the French are rendered helpless, but only that force of your beauty would be sung.]

So in the elegy to Boscán, Garcilaso soon apostrophizes Mars in a way that makes clear the antipathy of poetry to war: "O harsh, o severe, o fierce Mars, covered with a diamond tunic and forever hardened in every part! What can the tender lover"—that is, the elegiac poet—"do with your hardness and rough activity, always led on by fury?"

Turning back from these nearly contemporaneous poems to the sonnet from Carthage, we can hardly fail to recognize that its *arte italïano* as an art of war is deeply at odds with its *arte italïano* as an art of poetry. In poems like the elegy to Boscán, the elegy to Alba, the third eclogue, and the "Ode ad florem Gnidi," arms and the fury of Mars stand consistently *against* poetry and its interests, and such opposition is at least implicit in the epistle to Boscán. The imaginative freedom Garcilaso enjoys in that poem is freedom *from* his military and diplomatic duty. And the one poem, other than the sonnet to Boscán, that was written directly from the North African battlefield, the sonnet to Mario Galeota, wholly ignores the emperor's reasons for war and makes the enemy attack that in actual fact left Garcilaso wounded in the tongue and right arm Cupid's way of preventing his speaking and writing against the cruelty of love. Whatever may have been going on in the neighborhood of the fortress of Goleta from the perspective of Charles V and his troops on June 22, 1535, when Garcilaso the soldier received his wounds, a parallel skirmish involving Cupid, Garcilaso the lover, and the art of poetry was also

underway, and from the point of view of the poem only the second skirmish counts. By the time we reach its final tercet, the sonnet to Boscán
will take a similar turn, but even earlier in that poem, when both
Charles's conquest of Tunis and the ancient Roman destruction of Carthage dominate our awareness, remembrance of an *arte italïano*, an art
of poetry as well as an art of war, keeps open an alternative space—indeed, an oppositional space—that other poems Garcilaso wrote at this
time do so much to elaborate.

The word Garcilaso uses to bring memory into our consciousness—*reduzido* (led back) in the phrase *reduzido a la memoria el arte*—tells more of
the concrete nature of that alternative space. It is the space of other poetry and even other languages. *Reduzido* is, in the words of Daniel L.
Heiple, a "curious Latinism" whose use by Garcilaso is "modeled on the
first line of stanza 21 of [*Orlando furioso*] Canto 19: *Revocando a la memoria l'arte.*" As Ariosto "calls back" art to memory, so Garcilaso, prompted
by the North African victories of Charles V and armed with the Latin
verb *reducere,* "leads" it "back." Such interlinguistic and intertextual borrowing is central to the new poet's job of making his lowly vernacular
worthy of empire by making it foreign. He takes words from other languages and phrases from other poets to weave a splendid poetic fabric
that both is and is not Spanish, a poetic fabric that would make
Castillejo's troubadours gaze wonderingly *con ojos . . . de estranjeros.*

Herrera helpfully suggests the more positive value that might be attached to such innovation. Spotting another borrowing from Ariosto a
few lines farther down in the sonnet from Carthage, he has this to say:
"*Licenciosa.* A word that is elevated, meaningful, rotund, harmonious,
decorous, well-composed, solid and heroic in sound and worthy of being used often, and whoever denigrates it is guilty of ignorance; it is appropriate that this sublime term be used for a grand subject like this
one. . . . Ariosto in Canto 27 called a flame licentious, from where Garcilaso drew his inspiration." And elsewhere, commenting on a word Garcilaso has brought over from French, he says not only that "it is permissi-
ble for writers of one language to use words from another" but that it is
"very important" that they do so for with such foreign or "peregrine"
words "poems are ornamented and seasoned" and made to give "pleasure to those who read them." Now we are under no obligation to suppose that Herrera always speaks for Garcilaso. On the contrary, Garcilaso's courtly *sprezzatura* was far removed from the pedantic
seriousness of his commentator. But on these matters of art, Herrera ac-
curately defines the values Garcilaso put into practice. Garcilaso did
draw freely on other languages; he did use terms that brought an unac-
customed grandeur to Spanish; he did make Spanish new by making it
strange.

What both Herrera and Medina neglect in their enthusiasm for Garcilaso's art and their excitement over the support it brings to Spanish imperial arms is that for Garcilaso himself art and arms opposed rather than supported one another. The alienation of empire and the alienation of art were mutually dependent. Without the former there would have been no occasion for the latter. Empire deracinated men like Boscán and Garcilaso and transported them into a cultural space from which their native *coplas* and octosyllabics could only appear hopelessly inadequate. And for Garcilaso himself deracination took the still more literal form of official exile from Spain, exile that was relaxed only to allow for a few hasty diplomatic missions back to his Iberian homeland. Such exile led directly to the Roman turn his already Italianized art took. Nor did dependence go all one way. A deracinated art provided peregrine empire with the companionship it otherwise sorely lacked, as lyric poetry "became," in the words of Ignacio Navarrete, "the arena of the struggle for a modern cultural legitimacy independent of military conquest." Vernacular art, however far removed from its vernacular roots, gave homeless empire a national home.

Yet for all the practical dependence of art on empire and all the symbolic capital empire received in return, art seeks, as we have seen, a space apart from empire for its own self-reflection. With rare exceptions—most notable among them the opening eleven lines of the sonnet from Carthage but also the two initial tercets of the elegy to Boscán—Garcilaso's vernacular poetry either ignores empire or actively disavows it. Not "proud and wrathful Mars," not triumphant captains mounted on their chariots of war are his subject, but rather a "beautiful flower of Gnido" and the love she inspires. And even the two exceptions end by turning decisively away from imperial conquest. We have noticed this already with the elegy to Boscán. The mercenary motives of Garcilaso's fellow soldiers first deflect attention from the Scipio-like Tunisian victory of Charles V only to be dismissed in turn as a topic unfit for elegy, from which harsh, severe, and fierce Mars is similarly banished. As for the sonnet from Carthage, its engagement with empire is deeper than that of any other vernacular poem Garcilaso wrote, its sole rival being the Latin ode to Ginés de Sepúlveda, whose values are more those of Sepúlveda, the imperial propagandist, than of Garcilaso, the lyric poet. But that engagement, which can surely not be dismissed, is from the start shadowed by a competing engagement to an *arte italïano* whose profoundest identity is literary rather than military. And this is only the first of a series of rivals to empire the poem will reveal as we focus in turn on its *aquí*, on its *me deshago*, and finally on its *Boscán*.

4.
Aquí / Here

Aquí donde el romano encendimiento,
dond' el fuego y la llama licenciosa
solo el nombre dexaron a Cartago . . .

[Here, where the Roman conflagration, where fire and licentious
flame left only the name of Carthage . . .]

Garcilaso's sonnet from Carthage turns on a single word: *Aquí.* This
word and the tercet that follows from it are what have encouraged me to
ignore the title that has been affixed to the poem since its first appearance in print—"To Boscán from Goleta"—and refer to it instead as a
sonnet from Carthage. The usual title is in all likelihood an editorial addition. Never in the body of the poem does Garcilaso mention either
the fortress of Goleta or the conquered city of Tunis. Instead, his *aquí*
turns our attention momentarily away from the present, which in the
course of the opening eight lines had vied with the Roman past for
equal regard, and insists that we focus on the ancient destruction of Carthage. *Cartago,* as the last word in the tercet, reaches back across the
three lines to attach itself firmly to the tercet's first word, *Aquí. Aquí* is
Cartago. But why should that be so? Why should Garcilaso forget the
fortress of Goleta and the city of Tunis, the places Charles and his
armies had so recently and so triumphantly overrun, and remember
only that he is writing from a spot "where" over sixteen hundred years
earlier "the Roman conflagration, where fire and licentious flame left
only the name of Carthage"? A fuller answer must await the final tercet
with its introduction of Garcilaso's own present situation. But even before we read further, we need to pause over the "hereness" of Carthage.
If in the minds of sixteenth-century poets and humanists Rome stands
for empire, Carthage stands for all that empire destroys and strives to
leave behind. Thus for Garcilaso to insist on being in Carthage, to insist
that Carthage is his *aquí,* is to identify not with empire but rather with
places of which empire leaves only the name.

Place is the crucial term here. In its universalist ambition, empire is essentially placeless. The alienation I have noticed in both early modern empire and in the imperial art Garcilaso practiced is alienation from place. The far-flung empire of Charles V had no capital city. Even the symbolic capital city of Rome had fallen to an imperial sack, so that when a few years later Charles came to Italy for his formal coronation, he went instead to Bologna, a town with no greater claim to centrality than dozens of others. Nor did the emperor's continued physical presence establish what might be thought of as a de facto capital, for he rarely spent more than a few months at a time in any one place. And Garcilaso, first as a servant of the emperor and then as an exile, was scarcely less itinerant, scarcely less placeless.

Thinking along these lines, we might go so far as to read Garcilaso's death as the revenge of deeply rooted place against placeless imperial itinerancy. On September 19, 1536, marching with the emperor on an expedition through the south of France, Garcilaso and the others found their way blocked in the village of Le Muy by a dozen or so peasants who had stationed themselves in a tower overlooking a narrow bridge that provided the only passage through the village. According to an eyewitness account, "When the emperor heard it, he ordered [his soldiers] to go and find out who they were, and so some gentlemen went, asking them what they were doing there. They said it was their land and they were going to stay there; the gentlemen told them to come down out of the tower and go where they liked, and they answered that they did not want to leave the tower." Artillery was brought up and fired, opening a breach in the tower. Then several gentlemen, including Garcilaso, scaled the tower on a makeshift ladder. "While Garcilaso de la Vega and Captain Maldonado were going up, the men in the tower dropped a big, heavy stone, and it strikes the ladder and breaks it, and so [Garcilaso] and the Captain fell, and [Garcilaso] was badly wounded in the head, from which he died a few days later."

Among the many ironies in this fatal encounter, perhaps the most poignant is that, as a poet, Garcilaso not only repeatedly longed for death but that he also identified with the rootedness of people like the peasants who killed him. Such identification underlies his *Aquí . . . Cartago*. "Arms and the fury of Mars," the "strength and valorous hand" that leveled Africa "from end to end," "the Roman conflagration," "the fire and licentious flame"—these remain the proud accomplishments of all-conquering empire, and in this sonnet Garcilaso, whatever aversion he elsewhere expresses concerning military action, celebrates them. But he also selects as his own *aquí*, his own place, the Carthage of which Rome's violence has left only the name. Seen this way, Carthage might be taken to stand for other places overrun by empire, for Goleta and Tunis, for sacked Rome, for Mexican Tenochtitlán, for Inca Cuzco, and perhaps even for the village of Le Muy whose captured peasants were executed by the emperor's order. But of all such places the one to which Garcilaso would have been the most attached was his own home town of Toledo. Nor would such an association with Carthage have been particularly far-fetched. Arguing with regard to this same sonnet that "the comparison of antiquity and the Renaissance was hardly new," Daniel Heiple recalls that "in imitation of the Roman punishment of Carthage by razing the city and sowing salt in the earth, Charles implied such a comparison when he ordered the destruction of the 'casa solar' of the *comunero* Padilla family in Toledo (located very near Garcilaso's own house), and the sowing of salt in the ground." It would thus have been easy for Garcilaso and his Castilian readers to reverse the process and to have thought of Toledo when they read of ruined Carthage.

It is worth remembering what the revolt of the *comuneros* was about. The succession in 1516 of the young Charles of Ghent to the Iberian thrones of his grandparents Ferdinand and Isabella caused immediate concern. Would this Flemish prince who knew nothing of Spain respect the ancient rights and customs of the Spanish people? And when Charles arrived surrounded by Flemish advisers, many of whom he installed in positions of great power, the concern increased. Particularly galling was Charles's nomination as archbishop of Toledo and primate of Spain of an absentee Flemish boy, Guillaume de Croy, the nephew of Charles's widely hated counselor, the rapacious lord of Chièvres. Nor were the Spanish much pleased when their new king proposed to leave Spain, supported by their funds, to claim the imperial territories in Germany and Austria to which he had been elected following the death of his other grandfather, the emperor Maximilian I. In response to these provocations, the towns of Castile, led by Garcilaso's neighbor and distant kinsman Juan de Padilla and by his older brother Pedro Laso, rose up in opposition.

Among the events that most memorably marked the revolt in Toledo was a speech made by Pedro Laso. Addressing his fellow Toledan magistrates, Laso contrasts the peace, prosperity, and tranquillity of Spain at the time when Charles arrived from the Low Countries with "the complete confusion caused by the affronts, the audacity, and the greed of the Flemish, who have been sacking Spain for three years now." He then inveighs against "the robberies and offenses that they have perpetrated against our countrymen," pointing particularly to the foreigners' utter neglect of "native traditions" and their disregard "of our country's illustrious men" in the appointment to major offices. This latter abuse has, he says, "been made clearly manifest in the case of the archbishopric of Toledo, for which it is not customary, nor should it be, to entrust to anyone but a very respectable person. The Flemish have, however, given this post to a young foreigner who is entirely ignorant of our traditions, not so much so that he might govern the church of Toledo from very distant places through subordinates, but so that he might dispossess a city, a great region, and the richest part of Spain, and take the wealth to Flanders, which is what he is doing." Given this provocation and others like it, "it is incumbent upon all cities to head off these offenses," but it is especially the duty of Toledo "which is becoming something like the head of the whole kingdom." For this reason, he calls on his fellow councilmen to dispatch letters and messages warning "the other cities of the common danger and of the many wrongs that threaten us all, and to exhort them to see it fit to send delegates and lawyers." "Once the king is informed of all of these grievances by way of a public message," he continues, "he should be earnestly implored, first, that he not absent himself from Spain, and second, that he remedy the damages already caused." And if the king does not attend to these petitions, action will follow: "the cities should, in common accord, take whatever measures they feel most appropriate for the kingdom and the state." What we hear in this speech and what was made manifest in the revolt that did, in fact, follow from it is precisely the voice of place, of local traditions, local interests, and local rights, responding to the abuses of placeless empire. And it is a voice that comes from Garcilaso's own immediate family.

But, of course, when the armed conflict did break out, Garcilaso, as a member of the imperial guard, fought on the other side. He was wounded on August 17, 1521, at the battle of Olías, "when," according to his biographer Hayward Keniston, "the Toledans, who were in no small straits for provisions, came forth to scour the countryside," and he may have been present two months later for the surrender of Toledo and again another four months later when the widow of Juan de Padilla led a still further revolt from the house adjoining his own. All this does not, however, mean that he abandoned his identification with Toledo. Nor did his long absence from the city, including an extended period of formal exile, weaken his local allegiance. On the contrary, to the end of his life he writes very much as a poet of Toledo. This is particularly evident in what is probably his last poem, the beautiful third eclogue. Taken by his "stars" "far from [his] own land," he sings "of four nymphs who rose together from [his] beloved Tagus River," the river that nearly encircles Toledo. Artists in their own right, each of these nymphs embroiders with materials taken from the Tagus a scene of tragically thwarted love, the first three from Greco-Roman mythology and the fourth from Garcilaso's own first eclogue. The effect is to claim for the Tagus and for Spanish an ancient poetic legacy and to add to it a purely local story written by a poet of Toledo. Translation—both the translation of empire and the translation of learning—remains central to the new poetry. But that poetry must also insist on its own localism, on a particular place in which the translated culture is grounded and made new.

In the remarkable sonnet he wrote to the Italian poet Maria di Cardona, Garcilaso traces the whole circular process by which foreign inspiration produces a native art whose local riches then pay tribute to its foreign source.

> *Illustre honor del nombre de Cardona,*
> *décima moradora de Parnaso,*
> *a Tansillo, a Minturno, al culto Taso*
> *sujetto noble de imortal corona:*
>   *si en medio del camino no abandona*
> *la fuerça y el espirtu a vuestro Lasso,*
> *por vos me llevará mi osado passo*
> *a la cumbre difícil d'Elicona.*
>   *Podré llevar entonces sin trabajo,*
> *con dulce son que'l curso al agua enfrena,*
> *por un camino hasta agora enxuto,*
>   *el patrio, celebrado y rico Tajo,*
> *que del valor de su luziente arena*
> *a vuestro nombre pague el gran tributo.*

[Illustrious honor to the name of Cardona, tenth muse of Parnassus, you who for Tansillo, Minturno, and learned Tasso were a noble subject, immortally crowned: if in the middle of my journey, strength and spirit do not abandon your Laso, through you my daring steps will take me to the difficult summit of Helicon. From there, using the sweet song that controls the flow of water, I will easily be able to channel, by a course which had until now been dry, my native, celebrated and rich Tagus, so that the richness of its sparkling sand will pay great tribute to your name.]

Among the many features of this poem that deserve special mention is the initial sense of belonging to a distinguished Italian poetic community, centered on Maria di Cardona and including Luigi Tansillo, Antonio Minturno, and Bernardo Tasso. Given Tasso's high standing, there is a particular boldness in the rhyming of "Tasso" and "Laso." But for Garcilaso, the Italian inspiration that promises to lead his "daring steps . . . to the difficult summit of Helicon" will result not in an addition to Italian poetry but rather in a new course for Spanish, as Garcilaso's *camino* and the *camino* of the Tagus are made one. Nor does the local site have nothing of its own to contribute. The gold-laden sand of the

Tagus enriches all that flows through its newly redirected channel. No wonder then that in a sonnet on Garcilaso, Herrera says that for "Laso . . . the Tagus excels the rich Tiber and the pure Arno."

Identification with a specific place, often synecdochically identified with a neighboring river, is a recurring feature of the new poetry of sixteenth-century Europe, especially among those poets who write from a position of exile. A quick look at the three most significant of them—Camões, du Bellay, and Spenser—will give us a better sense of how the attachment to place functions in relation to the alienating attachments to empire and to art.

In *The Lusiads*, perhaps inspired by Garcilaso himself, Camões repeatedly invokes the nymphs of the Tagus, a river that runs from Garcilaso's Toledo across Spain and through Portugal to Camões's birthplace of Lisbon and to the Atlantic beyond. And in canto 7, "now banished, in hateful poverty, to long exile under alien roofs," he adds an invocation of the nymphs of the Mondego, the river that flows through Coimbra, where he was educated. This epic of imperial wandering, both on the part of its protagonist Vasco da Gama and on the part of Camões himself, who traveled even farther than his fifteenth-century hero, is thus firmly rooted in specific Portuguese places. And those places figure again in his sonnets. Though there is some question about the attribution of the sonnet addressed to the "Gentle waters of the Tagus" (*Brandas águas do Tejo*), its longing for the Tagus and its breathing of sighs in the airs of foreign lands and disturbing foreign waters with tears strikes a very Camonian note, while the unquestionably authentic "Sweet and clear waters of the Mondego" (*Doces águas e claras do Mondego*) makes the remembered place the basis of identity itself. As William Baer has recently translated the poem's second quatrain:

And now, I've gone away, sweet distant stream,
but, still, your memory overtakes me yet,
and never lets me change, or ever forget:
that the farther away I am, the closer I seem.

Like Garcilaso's eclogue and sonnet, Camões's epic and sonnets are foreign genres brought into the poet's vernacular as a way of radically refashioning it to meet the extraordinary demands of empire. The Tagus and the Mondego naturalize the borrowing, making the foreign familiar in much the way that Virgil's *Eclogues* and *Georgics* or Horace's talk of his Sabine farm do to the Greek forms those poets imported into Latin. What du Bellay's *Regrets* brings to the surface is the paradoxical preference for the distant site of memory and native identity even in the midst of an artistic enterprise that, except for the vernacular language itself, is wholly given over to foreign models. In what is probably his best known sonnet, the poem that begins *Heureux qui, comme Ulysse* (Happy the man who, like Ulysses), du Bellay envies the epic voyager who has "returned, full of wisdom and experience, to live among his kinfolk the rest of his life." Then, echoing Ovid's lament from his Pontine exile, he wonders when he "will again see smoke rising from the chimney of [his] little village."

There is irony already in the fact that du Bellay *in* Rome should borrow Ovid's nostalgic longing *for* Rome to express his own longing for his native Anjou. But the sonnet's final six lines increase the irony by making Rome, the ancient seat of empire, the explicit "other" against which the native place is valued.

> *Plus me plaist le sejour qu'on basty mes ayeux,*
> *Que des palais Romains le front audacieux,*
> *Plus que le marbre dur me plaist l'ardoise fine:*
> *Plus mon Loyre Gaulois, que le Tybre Latin,*
> *Plus mon petit Lyré, que le mont Palatin,*
> *Et plus que l'air marin la doulceur Angevine.*

(The home my ancestors built pleases me more than the grandiose facades of Roman palaces, fine slate pleases me more than hard marble, my Gallic Loire more than the Latin Tiber, my little Liré more than the Palatine hill, and more than sea air, the sweetness of Anjou.)

One might almost assume from this that du Bellay had abandoned the project he had defined in the *Defense*, the project of remaking French according to a Roman model. But that is not the case at all. This very sonnet is shot through with Roman echoes. Most of the poem's lines were even written in Latin before being brought over into French. What the poem does express is the need—a need shared with Garcilaso and Camões—for an *aquí* apart from the wandering and the glory of empire, a place to answer and to ground universal empire's inevitable estrangement.

So intense is that need that Spenser seized on the very place of exile, the Irish outpost to which he had been sent by the queen's government and made it a "home" to set against the distant imperial court. Some ambiguity does admittedly attend that crucial term in *Colin Clouts Come Home Againe*, the poem of Spenser's that most obviously engages the issues that have been interesting us. Is home the English court to which Spenser, after a long absence in Ireland, finally returns? Or is it rather the Irish countryside with which his pastoral persona now seems firmly identified? Though either reading is possible, the narrative weight of the poem strongly favors the second. The poem begins with Colin's rehearsal of the secret dalliance of the Bregog and the Mulla, rivers that run adjacent to Spenser's estate of Kilcolman in the Irish province of Munster, and it assumes throughout a position of distance from the Elizabethan court which Colin visits, admires, and deplores as a naive outsider, a figure whose primary attachment is to the pastoral world from which he came and to which he eventually returns. That Spenser was in fact a colonial planter, deeply implicated, as recent scholarship has shown, in some of the bloodiest acts of the English imperial regime in Ireland, makes evident, as does Garcilaso's divided allegiance with regard to African Carthage and his native Toledo, the profound inner conflicts that shape the new poetry of sixteenth-century Europe in whatever country it appears. Poetry of empire, it is also a poetry of place from whose perspective empire can seem anything but welcome.

Which brings us back to Garcilaso's *Aquí . . . Cartago.* Where one string of associations, the string I have followed so far, remembers Rome's destruction of Carthage in the Third Punic War and thinks of other places, Toledo among them, more recently reduced to submission by imperial "arms and the fury of Mars," another would recall an earlier Carthaginian conflagration, the self-immolation of Dido, and would turn from there to the ruined places of enchantment I evoked in the first chapter in discussing the most obvious self-contradictions of Renaissance epic. Those, too, the pleasure gardens of Ariosto's Alcina, Tasso's Armida, and Spenser's Acrasia, are places whose destruction is required by the onward progress of empire. *Delenda Carthago*, the elder Cato's repeated demand that "Carthage must be destroyed," might just as well be applied to each of these places of antiheroic sensual delight. I am not proposing that Garcilaso had any such places, other than Dido's Carthage, which he surely did remember, in mind as he wrote his sonnet. Only Ariosto's poem would have been available to him. But it is appropriate for us to think of them, for they are part of the tradition to which his poem contributes. When Melissa, the powerful anti-Alcina, appears to the enchanted Ruggiero in the person of his aged teacher Atlante, her sharpest rebuke is sarcastically to say, "This is certainly the high means by which we may hope that you may one day become an Alexander, a Caesar, a Scipio!" Becoming an Alexander, a Caesar, or a Scipio is the heroic ideal, the ideal of empire. Places that stand in the way of that ideal must be stripped of their enchantment, be made to disappear, or be brutally and utterly destroyed, a fate Spenser's Bower of Bliss shares with many real-world places from ancient Carthage to modern Rome, Tenochtitlán, Cuzco, and the *casa solar* of the Padilla family in Garcilaso's Toledo. But as they suffer that fate, we may find our sympathies unexpectedly shifting away from victoriously peregrine empire and toward the places empire so ruthlessly destroys.

5.
Me deshago / I am undone

buelve y rebuelve amor mi pensamiento,
hiere y enciend' el alma temerosa,
y en llanto y en ceniza me deshago.

[love turns and turns again my thought, wounds and inflames my
fearful soul, and in tears and ashes I am undone.]

Garcilaso's sonnet from Carthage consists of two sentences, each fit
neatly into one of the poem's two large metrical units. The first sen-
tence fills the poem's first eight lines, the octave; the second fills the final six lines, the sestet. But something of the extraordinary power of the
poem comes from its both stopping and not stopping at the octave-
sestet break. I have said that the poem turns on the single word *Aquí*.
That is both true and not true. *Aquí* narrows and sharpens the poem's
focus and invites us, particularly once we get to *Cartago*, to think of place
in the multiple ways I suggested in the previous chapter—place in opposition to the destructive headlong rush of empire. But the sestet's first
three lines also continue and accelerate the momentum of the octave,
as "arms and the fury of Mars" intensify into "the Roman conflagration"
and the "fire and licentious flame" that "left only the name of Carthage." Thus from the first line through the eleventh, Roman destruc-
tiveness, which in the octave has also an element of restorative power
that brings back to life the Roman Empire and back to memory the Italian art of Rome, expresses itself with increasing violence. This is a movement on two levels. In the opening lines we are most aware of the modern force of Charles V and his empire, but by the end of the octave and
then on into the first three lines of the sestet memory of ancient Rome
takes over. In these later lines it is Rome's leveling of Africa from end to
end in the Third Punic War and the brutal destruction of Carthage by
the younger Scipio Africanus that comes to dominate.

But in the last six lines as a whole, this memory of Rome sets the scene
for a similarly devastating action, though one that involves quite different actors. Here, where Scipio slaughtered the Carthaginians and burned

their city to the ground, "love turns and turns my thought again, wounds and inflames my fearful soul, and in tears and ashes I am undone." Like the ancient Carthaginians, like the modern inhabitants of Goleta and Tunis, Garcilaso is undone by a relentlessly imperious enemy. In an anagram much loved by Petrarch and sixteenth-century Petrarchists, *amor* takes the place of *Roma,* and a poem that had appeared to be an epic celebration of imperial might transforms itself as it "turns and turns again" into a lover's lamentation for his undoing.

In the context provided by the first eleven lines, this undoing resonates with associations that are hard to dismiss. Though Garcilaso came to Carthage as a soldier in an invading army, he ends by identifying with the victims of that army and even more particularly with the victims of that army's ancient Roman predecessor. Thinking of the Third Punic War and the younger Scipio's fiery destruction of Carthage, we may remember the wife of Hasdrubal, the Carthaginian general, who with her children threw herself into the flames rather than submit, as her husband had done, to Rome. And thinking of Carthage more generally and its legendary connection to the founding of Rome, we may also remember Queen Dido, who stabbed herself on a sacrificial pyre when her lover Aeneas left her to fulfill his imperial destiny. Neither of these identifications is made any more explicit in the poem than is the identification of Charles V with the two Scipios. But the insistence on the specific conditions of the Third Punic War points strongly toward the first, while the second is evoked not only by the conjunction of love, Carthage, and a death in tears and ashes, but also by a verbal echo in *hiere y enciende* of the "wound" and "fire" that afflict Dido in the opening lines of book 4 of the *Aeneid,* the book that ends with her suicide. Like Garcilaso, Dido has been struck by Amor, the son of Venus and half brother of Aeneas, and like both Garcilaso and Hasdrubal's wife, she ultimately falls victim to the cruel exigencies of empire.

Why would Garcilaso adopt the pose of the female African victims of Rome, the very empire he sees being reborn in the expedition of Charles V in which he fought? Why would he invite us to think of him as another Hasdrubal's wife, as another Dido? The lead provided by Herrera in his notes on this poem, though suggestive in other ways, does not get us very far. Herrera points to a much-imitated sonnet by Castiglione on the ruins of Rome, from whose opening lines, "*Superbi colli, et voi sacre ruine, / che'l nome sol di Roma anchor tenete*" (Proud hills, and you holy ruins, which only the name of Rome retain . . .), Garcilaso would seem to have taken the line *solo el nombre dexaron a Cartago,* as he perhaps took the *aterró* of line eight from Castiglione's *atterra* in his poem's eleventh line. Ruined but for a name, leveled by the forces that oppose them, Rome and Carthage, the victor and the vanquished, ultimately share the same fate, a reflection Garcilaso's borrowing makes available to those who notice it. But the precedent Castiglione's sonnet provides for Garcilaso's final tercet suggests difference as much as likeness. Both poets remember love, but where Garcilaso makes love a force bent on his destruction, Castiglione supposes that, like Rome, love and its pains will be worn away by time and, knowing that, he will henceforth live content in the hope of eventual relief. Thus, in the end, having our attention drawn to Castiglione's sonnet only makes Garcilaso's identification with the victims of empire appear more remarkable.

Sympathy with such victims was not, however, all that unusual. Anne J. Cruz, in a fine essay on the relations in sixteenth-century Spain between arms and letters, points to Garcilaso's own Latin ode to Juan Ginés de Sepúlveda on the Tunis campaign itself. Though the poem begins with a heroic image of the emperor, "mounted on his famous pied stallion, mov[ing] rapidly through the tight ranks, outrunning the swift wind, fervent as he brandishes the death-dealing lance in his hand," it quickly shifts attention to the Moorish wives, who "gaze from the high towers over the wide plains of the field," and sigh for their lovers "with a trembling breast." And though in this poem Garcilaso does not fully identify his voice with theirs, as he does in the sonnet, he does grant these women a quite astonishingly troubling speech of their own:

"O, young men," they cry, "avoid with your unequal strength the arms of Caesar and their abominable encounters. When to posterity his sacrificed mother gave his name, as they struggled to pull the weak infant from her womb, from this proceeds the Caesarean race, from this the delight in new slaughter: Do you think that he who from a funereal threshold thrust his savage foot into life would not derive from this and engender in others a native fury and a thirst for hot blood?"

Even here the new Caesar, Charles V, melds with the old, suggesting once again the rebirth of Rome. But what a birth it is! Like the whole Caesarean line, this new emperor "from a funereal threshold thrust his savage foot into life." From that murderously violent beginning, though Charles shares that beginning only metaphorically, he inherited a relish for "new slaughter" and an unquenchable "thirst for hot blood."

Unless we suppose that Sepúlveda was expected to glory in the bloodthirstiness of his sovereign, as he may well have done, he might seem an odd addressee for a poem that inspires such sympathy for the victims of empire. For some three decades, he was the chief proponent and apologist for the most aggressive and most contested actions of Charles's imperial and Spanish armies. The opening lines of Garcilaso's ode allude both to the treatise Sepúlveda had addressed to Charles urging him to attack the Turks and to the history he was to write of the Tunis campaign, a project that was to be based in part on the manuscript by Luis d'Ávila that Garcilaso was delivering and perhaps too on Garcilaso's own eyewitness account. But the justice of war on an Islamic rival was not Sepúlveda's only concern. He had also written to defend the sack of Rome as a well-deserved chastisement of papal corruption and pride, and he was soon to gain his greatest renown as the defender of Spanish actions in the New World against the vehement charges brought by Bartolomé de las Casas. That such a defense was urgently needed will be apparent to anyone who knows Las Casas's *Very Brief Account of the Devastation of the Indies*, where the savage taste for hot blood that Garcilaso's Moorish wives attribute to Charles V is shown over and over again to be characteristic of the Spanish conquistadors wherever they went. As for Rome, its sack occasioned a huge outpouring of accusations and lamentations. And even the conquest of Tunis, including particularly the poorly justified sack of the surrendered city, resulted in many expressions of sympathy beside Garcilaso's.

Though he was writing with the emperor's assistance and with the clear intention of winning the emperor's approval, such sympathy seems to have crept into Paolo Giovio's account of the expedition. When in 1550 Giovio sent the emperor the manuscript of this part of his history, Luis d'Ávila responded on behalf of the court that Giovio's account of the sack of Tunis was "so distinguished and efficacious . . . that I myself would have been almost overcome with pity for those people, had I not perceived by how great justice on the part of Caesar they were involved in the mournful fate of the city," and he goes on to insist that the people of Tunis were "unworthy of the lamentable commiseration to which you have moved the reader of your history." But despite the even closer surveillance that was exercised in the preparation of Jan Cornelisz Vermeyen's great series of tapestries on the Tunis expedition, "lamentable commiseration" for the victims of imperial power marks them as well. A scene of massacre that was part of Vermeyen's original drawing was replaced in the final version, but images that might be expected to arouse sympathetic emotion do survive into the completed work. Three are of particular note, all involving Moorish women and all in the prominent lower left-hand corner of their respective panel. One, which Hendrik J. Horn, the leading student of the tapestries, calls "the most rhetorical group of the entire . . . series," shows an old man, a woman, and a child mourning the fall of Goleta. Another, recalling the Roman soldiers at the Crucifixion throwing dice for Christ's garments, shows three imperial soldiers gambling for possession of a Moorish woman and child. And a third shows a soldier thrusting his musket into the back of a woman fleeing the sack of Tunis.

Yet, however intense, sympathy is not quite the same as the identification we find in the last lines of Garcilaso's sonnet from Carthage. Garcilaso does not merely sympathize with figures like Hasdrubal's wife or Dido. He becomes them. His voice merges with theirs. He ceases to be the imperial soldier he had been and becomes a victim of love who is as much Dido—and by the end of the poem Dido, rather than Hasdrubal's wife, is the dominant figure—as he/she is Garcilaso. Understood this way, Garcilaso's undoing—his *me deshago*—is not simply the familiar undoing of the lover as he dies from the unremitting cruelty of love, though it has certainly an element of that. It is also the undoing of the individual self, of the historical person of Garcilaso de la Vega, as he is absorbed into the transcendent self of the new poetry, a poetry whose best-known practitioners may be male but whose ultimate identity and source of inspiration is associated with such female figures as Dido.

Each of these undoings, the amorous and the poetic, recurs often in Garcilaso's poetry. Death from love is the constant preoccupation of his sonnets. The first talks obsessively of how his cruel mistress wants to *matarme, perderme, acabarme*—kill me, ruin me, bring an end to me—and each of the next thirteen play some variation on that theme, a theme that comes back in at least ten of the remaining twenty-six sonnets, as well as in several of the songs and in one of the two elegies. In a brilliant essay on Garcilaso's sonnet from Carthage—the only previous essay devoted wholly to this poem—José María Rodríguez García argues that "to dwell in Carthage," as Garcilaso does in this poem, "is to dwell in poetry." But it is also to dwell in death. More than empire, death is the poet's companion. To be made as a poet is, in this tradition, to be undone as man and lover. The poet's *me deshago*, which he shares with Dido and perhaps with Hasdrubal's wife, is the rite of passage by which he enters into the body of Western poetry, as that body was defined for the new poets.

A great many of Garcilaso's poems, in addition to the sonnet from Carthage, would serve to illustrate this dynamic of poetic making through personal and perhaps even physical unmaking, but two seem to me particularly resonant: sonnet 11 ("Hermosas nymphas") and sonnet 10 ("O dulces prendas"). In the first, Garcilaso addresses the lovely nymphs who live happily deep in the river in mansions built of shining stones upheld by crystal columns and who busy themselves embroidering fine fabrics and telling one another their loves and lives. The river is, in effect, the place of art, and the nymphs, like those who emerge from the Tagus in the third eclogue, are the artists of this watery otherworld. Standing on the bank of the river Garcilaso belongs to a different space, but he calls on the nymphs to lay their work aside and to raise their golden heads to look on him. In his sad state, it will not, he says, take long. "For either you will be sorry to listen, or else I will be changed to water by weeping here, and you will have plenty of time to console me down there." And what the poem describes, the suicidal melding of the poet into the deep waters of art, it also enacts. According to El Brocense and Herrera, Garcilaso draws for this poem on Virgil, Sannazaro, Petrarch, Geronimo Mucio, Claudianus, and Bernardo Tasso. As in the sonnet from Carthage, he undoes himself as an individual historical agent to remake himself as a new poet, a member of a transhistorical poetic community. Nor does the process stop with Garcilaso. Herrera works into his notes, as a way of joining this immortal company, a sonnet of his own on the Guadalquivir, the river that runs through his native Andalusia.

Still closer to the sonnet from Carthage is "O dulces prendas," for here Garcilaso's voice merges not just with that of poetic tradition but with that of Dido herself. Years earlier, in one of his eight surviving *coplas*, Garcilaso translated the final lines of Ovid's *Heroides* 7, Dido's epistle to Aeneas:

> *Pues este nombre perdí,*
> *"Dido, muger de Sicheo,"*
> *en mi muerte esto desseo*
> *que se escriva sobre mí:*
> *"El peor de los troyanos*
> *dio la causa y el espada;*
> *Dido, a tal punto llegada,*
> *no puso más de las manos."*

[Having now lost the name, "Dido, wife of Sichaeus," at my death I desire this to be written of me: "The worst of the Trojans supplied the cause and the sword; Dido, driven to such a point, applied to it no more than her hands."]

In this poem, Dido speaks for herself in words supplied first by Ovid and then translated by Garcilaso. Through this process, the poets imagine, as Virgil does in book 4 of the *Aeneid*, what it is like to be Dido. "O dulces prendas," like the sonnet from Carthage, goes still further. It adopts Dido's imagined voice as the poet's own. No longer impersonating her, it appropriates her as a version of the poet's self.

Here is how that extraordinary sonnet begins:

> *¡O dulces prendas por mi mal halladas,*
> *dulces y alegres quando Dios quería,*
> *juntas estáys en la memoria mía*
> *y con ella en mi muerte conjuradas!*

[O sweet souvenirs, found to my sorrow, sweet and happy as long as God so willed, you are all together in my memory, and conspiring with memory against my life!]

Mounting on her funeral pyre and seeing the Trojan garb and familiar bed she had ordered be placed there, Virgil's Dido, in her last speech before stabbing herself with Aeneas's sword, says, "O relics once dear, while God and Fate allowed, take my spirit and release me from my woes!" The imitation is obvious and was obviously meant to be seen. But the question remains. What does it mean for Garcilaso to take as his own Dido's dying words, as in the sonnet from Carthage he takes as his own her dying posture in tears and ashes?

Our earlier look at the heroic tradition can help supply an answer. To ask why Garcilaso chose to identify with Dido—in effect, to become Dido—is equivalent to asking why readers of the *Aeneid* find Dido so much more compelling than Aeneas, why both Surrey and du Bellay chose to translate book 4 of the *Aeneid* as the showpieces for their new vernacular poetics. As Lawrence Lipking puts it in his seminal book on the abandoned woman and poetic tradition, "Dido reveals the emptiness of empire." Nor is this an accidental feature of Virgil's poem. "Men in particular," Lipking argues, "seem incapable of voicing their darker passions except through the voices of women. . . . The male needs an abandoned woman to inhabit. . . . Apparently epics require abandoned women. . . . The *Aeneid* requires its Dido, if only to authenticate its hero's grief." As a poetry of empire, the new poetry of sixteenth-century Europe, including most conspicuously Garcilaso's own poetry, falls subject to these requirements. The revelation of empire's emptiness, poetry's longing to express darker passions, the need for an abandoned woman to inhabit, epic's quest for its abandoned other, the necessary authentication of heroic grief—these powerful undercurrents of the epic tradition surge to the surface in a poem like "O dulces prendas" or the final tercet of the sonnet from Carthage.

Rodríguez García sees in the sonnet from Carthage a struggle between epic and lyric that in the poem's final tercet lyric wins. Garcilaso chooses lyric over epic. But as Lipking's book makes clear and as our examination of the new poetry of empire affirmed, lyric is in this sense an inevitable part of epic. Imperial self-making necessarily entails a *me deshago*, an undoing that speaks for the victims of empire. Thus for Garcilaso's poetry to do the work Medina and Herrera expect of it, it must also undo that work. It must be both Scipio and Dido, both Rome and Carthage. A new poetry that clung only to imperial ambition, that celebrated even in a language modeled on that of Virgil and Horace only Rome and Rome's modern revival, that in effect ended with the eleventh line of Garcilaso's sonnet from Carthage would be so radically incomplete as to fail in the very enterprise it was single-mindedly pursuing.

I have said that the new poetry of sixteenth-century Europe is a poetry deeply at odds with itself. What Garcilaso's sonnet helps us see is that were this not so, were the contradictions somehow smoothed away, the compelling interest this poetry had for its contemporaries and continues to have for us would not survive. It is precisely because of the great rift between expectations that commentators like Medina and Herrera can acknowledge and those they cannot, precisely because Garcilaso is at once the celebrant of imperial revival, *and* the new poet, *and* the advocate of place, *and* the abandoned woman that his poetry achieves the cultural transcendence that makes of it something more than a partisan and historical curiosity. *Me deshago* thus necessarily completes "arms and the fury of Mars" as both are completed by *el arte italïano* and by *aquí*. These four engagements pull in quite different directions. They even contradict one another. But none of the four would have sufficed to give rise to either Garcilaso's sonnet from Carthage or to the new poetry of sixteenth-century Europe without the others.

Nor is our list of enabling conditions and commitments yet at an end. Neither "arms and the fury of Mars," nor *el arte italïano*, nor the native hereness of *aquí*, nor the self-immolation of *me deshago* would have found expression had Garcilaso been left to his own devices, for nowhere was the new poetry the product of unaided individual genius. Wherever it arose, it was, on the contrary, a collaborative undertaking— a collaborative undertaking whose complex inner dynamics Garcilaso's sonnet from Carthage does much to illuminate.

6.

Boscán / Boscán

Boscán . . .

In retrospect, whether in Spain, in France, or in England, the new poetry was seen as the work of not one but of two men. In his mocking appreciation of the estrangement of Castilian verse from its familiar patterns, Cristóbal de Castillejo credits both Boscán and Garcilaso. In Castillejo's fantasy, Boscán and Garcilaso together descend into the underworld where they meet up with the astonished troubadours of earlier Spanish poetry. Similarly, though with none of Castillejo's comic reservation, Michel de Montaigne praises both Pierre de Ronsard and Joachim du Bellay for having raised French verse "to the highest point it will ever attain," a point "scarcely removed from ancient perfection." And in England Samuel Daniel and many others recognized the unique contribution Philip Sidney and Edmund Spenser had made to the renovation of English verse. Together they "presume of fame / And seem to beare downe all the world with lookes." Others were of course involved. Boscán and Garcilaso got their initial prompting from Andrea Navagero and Garcilaso especially had much additional encouragement from the community of humanists in Naples. Jacques Peletier du Mans first suggested that du Bellay and Ronsard try the sonnet and the ode; Jean Dorat provided both with a rigorous training in classical studies at the College of Coqueret; and a group of like-minded friends clustered around them as the other members of the Pléiade. With the Areopagus, Sidney and Spenser had their own "senate" of friends ready to lay down laws for a new English poetry, and with Roger Ascham's *Schoolmaster* they had a prompting—a misguided prompting, as it turned out—as to what form those laws should take. But however many friends and mentors were involved, in each country a core couple emerged as the prime agents of change.

Now I do not suppose that there is any necessity in this arrangement. But it has occurred often enough—and not only in sixteenth-century Spain, France, and England—to suggest that radical cultural change favors such a configuration—or, perhaps better, that such a configuration favors radical cultural change. Why that might be so is suggested by Boscán's letter to the duchess of Soma, written long after Garcilaso's death. Talking of the difficulty he encountered when he first tried composing poetry in Italian meters and Italian genres, Boscán says that the modest success he began having "would not have been enough to spur me very far had its value not been confirmed by Garcilaso, whose judgment is trusted as a true measure not only in my opinion but in that of everyone. And thus, many times praising my project and closing the matter by approving it with his own example, for he also intended to follow this path, he supported the task that occupied my moments of leisure. And soon, now that his urging freed my judgment, reasons occurred to me every day to take what I had begun even further." Garcilaso provided what Boscán most needed, not just encouragement but also collaboration. And the opposite must also have been true. Boscán provided the lead Garcilaso needed to get started and the collaboration he needed to keep going.

The very intensity of such friendship—the two of us against the world—lends the rare energy to their shared enterprise that we hear echoed a decade and a half later in Boscán's memory of reasons occurring to him "every day to take what I had begun even further." Something of the same note is sounded in the preface to Ronsard's first book of *Odes* where he talks of how he had been urged into print by "Joachim du Bellay, whose judgment, similar study, long acquaintance, and ardent desire to awaken French poetry, prior to us weak and languishing . . . , has made us nearly identical in spirit, invention, and work." And though Spenser would never have dared to claim identity with Sidney—the social distance between them was too great for that—a similar excitement about the poetic enterprise they shared, the attempt to remake English verse according to the quantitative measures that had governed Greek and Latin, animates the letters he wrote Gabriel Harvey from Leicester House where both he and Sidney were living. And about the same time Spenser dedicated his major self-presentational work, his *Shepheardes Calender*, to Sidney, who was just then working in a similar pastoral vein. Would the sonnets and *canciones* of Boscán and Garcilaso, the sonnets, odes, and the *Deffence et illustration de la langue françoyse* of Ronsard and du Bellay, the pastoral works with their extraordinary range of metrical experiments of Sidney and Spenser have been written without their having been part of a collaborative enterprise? It seems unlikely. If innovation does not require company, it certainly benefits from it. Two can more easily transform a national literary culture than one. One risks being regarded as little more than an anomaly. Two provide the core of a movement.

But such innovative pairs generally—perhaps necessarily—have their own internal hierarchy. Spenser writes with pleasure that Sidney and his friend Edward Dyer had him "in some use of familiarity," and he hails Sidney as "the president / Of noblesse and chevalrie" under the shadow of whose wing he flees for "succoure." Sidney's only surviving reference to Spenser is the acknowledgment in his *Defense of Poesy* that Spenser's *Shepheardes Calender* "hath much poetry in his eclogues, indeed worthy the reading." That Spenser had him in some use of familiarity was not an honor Sidney would have thought worth advertising, nor would he have considered seeking succor under the shadow of Spenser's wing. And though the relationship between Ronsard and du Bellay was much closer—du Bellay calls Ronsard "half my soul"—and much more extensively documented, hierarchy marks it as well.

Du Bellay may have led the Pléiade into battle with his militantly offensive *Deffence et illustration de la langue françoyse*, but Ronsard was always recognized, as he still is today, as the Pléiade's chief. And that recognition along with an obsessively repeated admission of Ronsard's superior accomplishment is a continuing theme of du Bellay's poetry. Ronsard, he says, holds "the highest place in the Aonian troop." Even during his lifetime, Ronsard enjoys the undying honor he deserves. Victory is his. Already triumphant laurel crowns his head. While du Bellay and his miserable fellows struggle unavailingly to find a way out of Hades, Ronsard revels in the bliss of Elysium. Such preeminence is, furthermore, well deserved, for Ronsard has made "French the equal of Greek and Latin." All that remains for du Bellay is to "imitate, if I can, the humblest songs of your weary Muse." The very excess of these statements and others like them hints at a sometimes jealous rivalry that was certainly part of du Bellay's feeling toward his friend. But still one could no more imagine Ronsard writing of du Bellay the way du Bellay wrote of him than one could imagine a similar reversal between Sidney and Spenser. Though we may now think Spenser a greater poet than Sidney and though at least some critics are inclined to prefer du Bellay to Ronsard, the ranking within each of these two couples was at the time of their collaboration unmistakable. Sidney and Ronsard were the leaders; Spenser and du Bellay, the emotionally dependent followers.

Making comparable remarks about Garcilaso and Boscán may at first appear considerably more difficult. On neither side do we find one sheltering under the protective wing of the other or announcing the other's greater accomplishment. Yet though the distinctions are more subtle, they do exist and are no less emotionally fraught. This is particularly so in the moment that most interests us, the moment of the Tunis expedition. If in his sonnet from Carthage, Garcilaso takes on the guise of the abandoned woman, who has abandoned him? Several candidates spring to mind. Inasmuch as he has assumed the role of Dido, we could say that Aeneas has done the abandoning. From that perspective, Garcilaso has been abandoned and consequently undone by the quest for empire itself. Biographical critics would, however, have other answers. They would point to the death in 1533 or 1534 of Isabel Freire, the woman who is sometimes thought to have inspired much of Garcilaso's verse and whose death is lamented in his first and third eclogues. Or they might favor the anonymous Neapolitan mistress whose imagined infidelity sparks the jealousy that inflames the elegy he was to write a month or so later to Boscán. But what of Boscán himself? When we read the sonnet from Carthage, particularly alongside the other two poems Garcilaso addressed to his friend in these months, it is difficult to ignore the urgency of the appeal made by all three poems. Nor is it easy to dismiss the personal implications of this appeal. When Garcilaso cries out, *Boscán . . . me deshago,* as he does in the sonnet from Carthage, it is as much with a sense of Boscán's responsibility for his plight as it is with that of Dido's Aeneas or the presumed, though shadowy, love objects of his other poems, whether Isabel Freire or the mistress in Naples. The love Garcilaso most intensely cherishes, the support he most insistently craves, and the abandonment he most fears are, quite simply, those of Boscán.

No such asymmetrical dependence marks the early evidence of their friendship. Boscán and Garcilaso seem to have first met shortly after Garcilaso joined the royal court in 1520. Boscán was by that time the *ayo,* or mentor, in courtly and chivalric behavior to the young Don Fernando Alvarez de Toledo, the future duke of Alba. Garcilaso's friendship with Don Fernando and with Fernando's kinsman Don Pedro de Toledo no doubt bound him still more closely to Boscán, whose role in Don Fernando's education Garcilaso celebrates in his second eclogue. "Anyone could judge by his manner," he writes of Boscán, "seeing his gestures full of wise, honest, and sweet grace, that he was a man perfected in the finer parts of the difficult art of courtesy, the mistress of sweet and civilized life. . . . It was he who had given Don Fernando his social grace, his upbringing and gentility, his sweetness and easy sincerity, his singular and generous virtue, and essentially anything of courtliness with which it was evident Fernando's heart was amply furnished, by forming his character with continuous example." The two *coplas* that feature Boscán echo as well the courtly setting of their friendship and its fully reciprocal nature. In the first Garcilaso humorously answers a verse by Boscán about the dancing of a mutual friend, and in the second Garcilaso jokes about Boscán's own dancing at some weddings in Germany.

That Boscán and Garcilaso were together in Germany suggests that both were involved in the campaign in 1532 to relieve Vienna from the

Turkish menace, a campaign led by the duke of Alba. A decade earlier both participated along with Don Pedro de Toledo in the fruitless attempt to rescue Rhodes from the Turks, and both would seem to have taken part in 1524 in an expedition against the French in Pamploma. As a further sign of their friendship and its coincidence with the imperial enterprises that defined the lives of both, Boscán was among the witnesses of Garcilaso's 1529 testament, which he made in Barcelona while traveling to Italy for the emperor's coronation, an event that may have engaged Boscán as well.

But sometime shortly following the Austrian expedition, things changed for both Garcilaso and Boscán. While Garcilaso, as part of his continuing exile from Spain, was stationed at the viceregal court in Naples, Boscán ceased his regular attendance at court and his participation in imperial military and ceremonial ventures. Instead he retired to his home in Barcelona, where he was soon to marry Ana Girón de Rebolledo. To Boscán's retirement may be credited his translation of *The Book of the Courtier*. According to the prefatory letters both Boscán and Garcilaso addressed to Doña Gerónima Palova de Almugáver when the book was published in April 1534, it was in the preceding year that Garcilaso sent Boscán a copy of the book, which had been published five years earlier in Venice, and urged him to translate it, and it was on one of his brief diplomatic visits to Spain—the only allowed breaks in his exile—that Garcilaso helped oversee the final revision of the translation, whose style he so warmly applauded. As a further consequence of his retirement, Boscán did not join the Tunis expedition of 1535, an absence to which we owe the three poems Garcilaso sent him: the blank-verse epistle of October 1534, the sonnet from Carthage of July 1535, and the elegy of August 1535. And in these three poems, Garcilaso's dependence on the friend he had in some ways left behind becomes apparent.

Well after the death of Garcilaso, Boscán, who seems never to have addressed a poem to his friend in his lifetime, included a stanza on Garcilaso in his *Octava rima*. The stanza celebrates Garcilaso as a poet of love and ends with this exclamation: *¡O dichoso amador, dichoso amado, / que del Amor acrecento el estado!* (O fortunate lover, fortunate beloved, who has enlarged the realm of Love). Given the quantity and variety of Garcilaso's love poetry, it is hazardous to attach this praise to any particular poem, but if there is any to which it applies more than to any other it would be to the epistle Garcilaso addressed to Boscán himself—the *dichoso amado*—for it is in this poem that he most clearly defined the character of love and the pleasure he takes in loving, here that he most obviously enlarges the realm of Love. But, it will be objected, this is a poem of friendship not of love. And it is true that Garcilaso begins talking of *amistad* and that, as Herrera pointed out, he draws heavily on Aristotelian ideas of friendship. But as he proceeds, *amor* takes the place of *amistad* as the poem's key term, and the intensity of the feeling he expresses is difficult to confine within the usual bounds of friendship.

The poem does, however, begin with "perfect friendship" granting a "free and pure informality" that befits the Horatian epistle. But then, as Garcilaso allows "freer and looser rein" to his fancy, his thoughts deepen.

One day, as I rode along considering the benefits of all who have, with outstretched hand, shown the way of friendship, and you, who exemplify friendship, at once came to mind; with you at least one great and apparently extraordinary thing happens to me: to tell you in a few lines, it is, that considering the benefits, honors, and pleasures that come to me from your friendship, which I hold so dear, I nevertheless count as still more valuable, nor does anything give me more sweet felicity, than the love I feel for you. This holds me so strongly that though well aware of the other aspects of our friendship and closeness, my soul is moved by this alone; and I know that here delight profits me as nowhere else, for it is usually put off for more useful and serious things. Continually seeing its forceful effect makes me examine its cause, and I discover that the benefit, distinction, joy, and pleasure that come to me from this loving tie with which our nature has bound our hearts are things that do not extend beyond myself, and in myself alone the benefit is made known. But love, from which fortunately all things are born, including any that might serve your use and pleasure, is itself reason enough for me to hold it in higher esteem than anything else, for how much more noble and virtuous it is to do good than to receive it; thus I delight in loving, and find that my delight is no folly.

I quote at length because this seems to me a remarkably telling passage, one that provides strong evidence of the asymmetry of this relationship. Where the somewhat tepid gifts of "friendship," "benefits, honors, and pleasures," come to Garcilaso from Boscán, what Garcilaso feels in return is "love," a love that finds satisfaction not so much in reciprocity—there seems to be little expectation of that—but rather in its own expression: "in myself alone the benefit is made known." It is as though Garcilaso wanted both to confess his love and to free Boscán of the embarrassment of any implication of feelings stronger than those of friendship on his side. This love is a good Garcilaso performs but does not receive. "Thus I delight in loving, and find that my delight is no folly." But, still, even with these qualifications, the potential for embarrassment is great enough that he then immediately changes the subject with a revealing phrase—"O how ashamed and sorry I am"—and jokes of the poor roads and inns of France only to end with a safely conventional allusion to Petrarch and Laura.

Suggestive as this poem is, it can hardly match the bizarre fervor of the elegy to Boscán that provides the other frame for the sonnet from Carthage. Writing from Sicily on his return from Tunis, Garcilaso briefly evokes the military triumph in which he had participated and mocks the sordid material motives of his fellow soldiers only to reproach himself for slipping into satire when what he means to write is an elegy, a form that he understands as devoted to lamentation. And what has he to lament? The wholly imagined infidelity of a sketchily defined mistress he left behind in Naples, "the land of the Siren." The cause seems hardly adequate to justify the intensity of the emotions that result from it, not only raging jealousy but also shame and suicidal despair. Indeed, it would be difficult, unless one takes this as merely a conventional exercise in the extremity of love, to imagine a situation adequate to explain the strength of the feelings expressed. And why should all this be addressed to Boscán? Why should he, rather than the supposed beloved, be the privileged recipient of these searing confidences? Nor is it simply a matter of Boscán's name being affixed to the poem's first line and then his presence as chosen auditor being forgotten. On the contrary, in the very moment when Garcilaso imagines himself ending like one "who in a warm bath dies without feeling it, having gently opened his own veins," he thinks of Boscán. "You, in your native land, among those who love you well, looking at the delightful shore and hearing the sound of the sea that breaks on it and gazing without hindrance upon her to whom you are granting eternal fame in your lively writings, rejoice, for a more beautiful flame than that which the burning of Troy made inflames your heart; you have no need to fear the contrary movement of fortune, for a pure splendor calms the wind."

How are we to take these contradictory, yet juxtaposed passages? One of my graduate students had an immediate answer when the question came up in class. "Threatened suicide and jealous admiration are parts of a familiar pattern. I'm dying while you are enjoying life and love with someone else. The real beloved is Boscán, and Garcilaso is desperately appealing for his attention and sympathy." How plausible is this suggestion? It can certainly not be confirmed in any more than a speculative way, and it is actively denied by the allusion to a mistress in the land of the Siren. Yet it does more easily explain the passionate extremity of the poem and its address to Boscán than does the notion of a hypothetically unfaithful mistress in Naples. If absence is, as he says, what prompts Garcilaso to suspect infidelity, he had been absent from Boscán far longer than the two months he had been away from Naples. And famously uxorious, newly married Boscán did in fact have a lover, his wife Ana Girón, who was consuming his attention and his poetry. Though the pattern of movement reverses that of the *Aeneid*—Garcilaso has departed in response to the claims of empire and Boscán has stayed behind—it is Garcilaso who assumes the role of the abandoned lover, Garcilaso who sounds like Dido. And so he ends the elegy insisting on the inescapability of his suffering, and "from this living fire in which I am purified and hope to be consumed little by little"—think of Dido on her funeral pyre—"I know that even there I will not be safe, and thus torn between extremes I die."

"Thus torn between extremes I die." "And in tears and ashes I am undone." The last words of the elegy to Boscán and the last words of the sonnet from Carthage, also addressed to Boscán, are similar enough to suggest a deep commonality between the two poems. If the elegy cries out Dido-like to Boscán, so too does the sonnet. What is certainly true of all six of the poems Garcilaso wrote during the months of the Tunis expedition is not only that each has a particular addressee but also that the identity of the addressee is central to the meaning of the poem. However we may finally decide to read them, the epistle and elegy to Boscán would necessarily be very different poems were they addressed to anyone else. Similarly the sonnet to Mario Galeota, the elegy to the duke of Alba, and the Latin ode to Ginés de Sepúlveda are specific in topic and tone to the man to whom each is addressed. Only with the sonnet from Carthage might we ignore, as critics have routinely done, the address to Boscán. But that would be as much a mistake with this poem as with any of the others. As a fellow courtier and soldier in the entourage of Charles V, Boscán shared Garcilaso's interest in "arms and the fury of Mars" and the role they played in restoring the Roman Empire. As a fellow new poet, he shared too the devotion to the revival of an "Italian art" in letters as well as in arms. As a student of Virgil and a patriotic native of Barcelona, who understood Garcilaso's attachment to Toledo, he could be expected to respond to the sonnet's *aquí* and the full implications of that *aquí* relative to the countervailing demands of universalist empire. And as the love object evoked in Garcilaso's blank-verse epistle and perhaps in the elegy as well, he was an appropriate addressee for the final *me deshago*, however he might have chosen to take it.

As it happens, Boscán did write a sonnet to Garcilaso after the latter's death that evokes in its own way the theme of abandonment.

> *Garcilasso, que al bien siempre aspiraste*
> *y siempre con tal fuerça le seguiste,*
> *que a pocos passos que tras él corriste,*
> *en todo enteramente l' alcançaste,*
>
> *dime: ¿por qué tras ti no me llevaste*
> *cuando de 'sta mortal tierra partiste?*
> *¿por qué, al subir a lo alto que subiste,*
> *acá en esta baxeza me dexaste?*

Bien pienso yo que si poder tuvieras
de mudar algo lo que 'sta ordenado,
en tal caso de mí no t' olvidaras:

que, o quisieras onrrarme con tu lado.
o a lo menos de mí te despidieras;
o, si esto no, después por mí tornaras.

[Garcilaso, you who always aspired to virtue and pursued it with such strength, who always ran after it only a few steps behind, you have now entirely achieved it in every way. Tell me: Why did you not take me with you? When you departed from this mortal earth to ascend the heights, why did you leave me in this base world? I am quite convinced that if you could have changed anything from what is ordained, you would not have forgotten me. You would want to honor me by letting me be at your side, or at least you would have said good-bye, or if not that, you would soon have returned for me.]

From this one might suppose that in the face of Garcilaso's death and the infinitely greater accomplishment of his poetry, which Boscán might by then have begun to recognize, the hierarchy of dependence would have reversed itself and Boscán would have felt something of the need for Garcilaso that Garcilaso once felt for him. But the poem is itself too flat and commonplace, too little animated by the kind of passion we find everywhere in Garcilaso, to sustain such a reading. Not even here can Boscán enter more than formally into the fabric of the greatest new poetry toward which his and Garcilaso's adoption of Italian meters and Italian and Roman forms aspired.

But Boscán did do something that in the history of Spanish poetry counted for no less. After having shown Garcilaso the way and after having sustained him with his active collaboration, Boscán saw that Garcilaso's poems were collected and published. And for that, more than for his own verse, his name still resonates in Spanish letters. Taken as a whole, the mutual dependence between Boscán and Garcilaso is at least as great as that between any two poets responsible for the various new poetries of sixteenth-century Europe. The accomplishment of neither would have happened without the other. Without Boscán, Garcilaso might never have attempted the Italianate verse that provides the basis for his poetic career. And without Garcilaso, Boscán would not only have lacked the encouragement to persevere in the course he had undertaken but his poetry would also have lacked its enabling association with a much more distinguished body of verse. Boscán helped make Garcilaso a new poet, and Garcilaso has helped keep Boscán famous.

What the sonnet from Carthage and the other two poems Garcilaso addressed to Boscán during the months surrounding the Tunis expedition add to this is an insight into the rare emotional complexity, at least on Garcilaso's side, of this relationship. Not that the relations of Spenser to Sidney and of du Bellay to Ronsard were not complex. They were. In each case there was a dependence of one on the other that is essential to the very emergence of a new vernacular poetry in the respective countries and languages of each. But Garcilaso's appeal to Boscán enters into the deepest substance of his poetry, into the *me deshago* that is so characteristic of this death-haunted poet. If, in the sonnet from Carthage, Garcilaso takes on the voice of Dido in her last minutes, his address to Boscán, particularly when that address is understood from the dual perspective of the epistle and of the elegy to Boscán, suggests that Boscán is himself deeply implicated in that poetic self-immolation. Put most bluntly, as abandoned woman, Garcilaso most fears the abandonment of Boscán, and that fear gives his poem a passionate fervor it would otherwise lack.

But there is a danger in focusing too insistently on what precisely Garcilaso may have meant in addressing Boscán in these three poems. The very extravagance of his feelings risks deflecting our attention from the larger point as it concerns the new poetry generally. As much as the new poetry is committed to empire, to art, to place, and to erotic undoing, so it is committed to the homosocial bonds of male friendship and male collaboration. Even at its most solipsistic, even when, as in the final tercet of the sonnet from Carthage, the lover poet seems utterly isolated from the great public enterprises of empire, art, and communally shared place, this is still poetry addressed to another man. And, more than that, it is poetry made with other men. Against the alienation of empire, in some way produced by the alienation of empire, stands the solidarity of male fellowship, the solidarity of men brought together by their removal from home and family and directed toward the common undertaking of a new poetry by that very removal. That such solidarity has its own tensions, its own jealousies, its own inadequately requited desires only points to its vitality. Like the other commitments that underlie and enable the new poetry, the commitment to male fellowship can be complexly self-contradictory. But, as with the others, that is what made it so richly productive. Changing the world, including the world of poetry, does not happen without conflict between commitments and also within them.

Epilogue: Poetry of the New

How does it happen that a single sonnet can be made to stand for and even anticipate a literary movement that had begun less than a decade earlier in Spain and that in the coming decades was to spread through much of western Europe? Would just any poem do? Is the whole contained in each of its parts as the genetic material of a whole organism is found in each of its cells? In some way that may be the case. In its metrical and generic form, in its diction and figurative language, in its alienation from earlier vernacular poetry, every example of the new poetry, including all the post-*coplas* work of Boscán and Garcilaso and all the extant poetry of Ronsard, du Bellay, Sidney, and Spenser, to say nothing of the work of their legion of imitators, speaks of the whole far-flung international movement of which it is part. In that sense almost any poem *would* do.

But in another sense Garcilaso's sonnet from Carthage is unique. I know of no other poem, certainly no other poem of comparable brevity, that would invite so comprehensive a discussion of the most fundamental engagements of the new poetry wherever it occurs, no other poem that speaks at once of ancient and modern empire, of a renewed Italo-Roman art, of the specificity of place and its claims, of the self-annihilating demands of love, of the emotionally fraught friendships and collaborations from which the new poetry arose. And not even this poem would do all this unaided. To realize in any adequate way the full implications of these engagements, we need to put, as I have been doing throughout this essay, the sonnet from Carthage in the company of Garcilaso's other poems, of poems by other poets, including some who wrote long after Garcilaso, and of other texts of all sorts in a great circular movement in which various points on the circle are made to illuminate one another. But however dependent our reading is on other materials, it nevertheless returns to Garcilaso's sonnet from Carthage as to its base, the one place where all the vital engagements are made known and function in a dynamic poetic relation to one another. Here alone, to retrieve a metaphor from this essay's preface, the whole ecology of the new poetry can be seen at work within the scope of just fourteen lines.

Why should this be the case? What made this poem the unique epitome that I am supposing it to be? Most important, the sonnet was written by a great poet working at the top of his bent. This is proven by the extraordinary body of work that belongs to these months, including most obviously the five other poems that coincide with the Tunis expedition, but extending a few months on either side to embrace the "Ode ad florem Gnidi," the three eclogues, and perhaps even a few of the most closely related sonnets like "Hermosas nymphas" and "O dulces prendas." These are poems that easily surpass any that had before been written in Spanish (or, in the case of the ode to Ginés de Sepúlveda, any written by a Spaniard in Latin), poems whose command of metrical forms and power of expression would only a few years earlier have appeared unthinkable.

But other conditions weigh more specifically on this particular poem. The Tunis expedition itself with its clear recollection of the Roman triumphs of the Punic Wars and of the Virgilian encounter with Dido is the most obvious of these. If this is an occasional poem, the occasion could hardly have been more richly suggestive. Still vivid memories of the *comuneros* revolt and other memories, though undoubtedly less vivid in Garcilaso's mind, of the sack of Rome and the conquest of Tenochtitlán and Cuzco also played their part. So, too, did Garcilaso's involvement with the humanist community in Naples, an involvement that made him see and seize on possibilities in the new poetry that went well beyond the Petrarchan limits that had hitherto confined his experiments. In Naples, *el arte italïano* came to mean far more than it had when Boscán and Garcilaso began their joint remaking of Spanish poetry. And there was also the relation with Boscán and the pressure brought to bear on it by Garcilaso's exile and Boscán's marriage. Without that, the poem would hardly have begun and ended as it does: *Boscán . . . me deshago.*

Intertextuality also has its share in making the sonnet from Carthage the remarkable epitome that it is. The poem announces its epic ambition by opening with a reminder of the opening line of Virgil's *Aeneid*, and it closes echoing the great anti-epic moment of the *Aeneid*, the death of Dido. And along the way from Virgilian beginning to Virgilian ending, it twice borrows from the greatest modern heroic poem, Ariosto's *Orlando furioso*. Nor are epic remembrances the poem's only intertextual features. In recalling that Rome left only the name of Carthage and leveled (*aterró*) Africa from end to end, it borrows conspicuously from Castiglione's famous sonnet on the ruin of Rome itself, a poem whose many imitators included a near translation by Gutierre de Cetina that substitutes Carthage for Rome. Was Cetina reading Castiglione through the lens of Garcilaso? It is impossible to say. But in the much broader way that it has been the business of this essay to point out, Garcilaso's sonnet from Carthage anticipates without specifically influencing the whole of the new poetry throughout sixteenth-century Europe and beyond.

So what is the new poetry? It is first and most conspicuously "movement" poetry that self-consciously sets out to impose a program of literary renewal on the literature of its particular vernacular. The French with the *Deffence et illustration* of du Bellay followed by innumerable prefaces and poetic declarations provide the most obvious example, and the English with Spenser's *Shepheardes Calender* and Sidney's *Defense of Poesy* are not far behind. The Spaniards, who came first, beat the drum a little less loudly. Their manifesto, Boscán's letter to the duchess of Soma, was written after the fact and appeared only posthumously, but the poems themselves, including Garcilaso's sonnet from Carthage, make clearly if more subtly their own declaration of difference.

Second, as befits the proclamations that accompanied them, the actual poems of these new poets are deliberately and strikingly unlike anything that had previously appeared in their respective languages. Garcilaso's sonnets, *canciones*, elegies, epistle, and eclogues, Ronsard's odes, du Bellay's sonnet sequences, Spenser's eclogues and chivalric romance, Sidney's pastoral romance and sonnet sequence could all claim—and most did claim—to be the first of their kind in their language. Nor did innovation stop with the introduction of novel generic forms. In all three countries, new meters and new stanzaic forms held an essential place in the enterprise. Spenser and Sidney's struggle, advertised in the Spenser-Harvey correspondence, with quantitative meter have in this regard more successful counterparts in Boscán and Garcilaso's adoption of Italianate hendecasyllabics as what then became the standard metrical form of Spanish poetry and Ronsard and du Bellay's revival of the long-neglected alexandrine as the basic French line, one that continued to dominate French poetry for the next three and a half centuries. And with the exception of the alexandrine (which Ronsard defined as the French equivalent of Greek and Latin heroic verse) and Spenser's recovery of archaic English diction (a recovery that had its own precedent in Virgil), the new poets went abroad—to ancient Greece and Rome or to modern Italy—in search of their novelties.

Why this series of radical departures? There are many reasons for it, but, as I have already suggested at length, one shared from country to country was an acute sense that the imperial ambitions of their respective nations, their desire to become in their time what Rome had been in its, required a poetry more like Rome's, required that they do what the Romans themselves had done in imitating the Greeks. Antonio de Nebrija's declaration that "language has always been the companion of empire" defined a program that both prompted and justified the efforts of vernacular writers throughout Europe. But the very fact that these were vernacular writers, writers working in the local idiom of a particular place, introduced a tension between the universalist aspirations of empire and more narrowly national ambitions. Had the imperial design been fully realized, whether in Spain, France, or England, there would have been a need for only one new poetry, for only one linguistic companion of empire. But that is not what happened. Instead several monarchic states claimed for themselves imperial status in the sense of absolute sovereignty and several new poetries developed in support of those claims. The new poetry is thus at once imperial and national, universal and local, singular and multiple.

And, as we have seen, the new poetry is at odds with itself in another still more profound way, for when we think of what these ambitious young poets of empire and nation actually wrote, an unavoidable anomaly immediately emerges. The one import they all share is not a genre taken from Greece or Rome but rather the Italianate sonnet, and when they do borrow other genres they are likely to fill them with sonnetlike material. What then can the solipsistic poetry of erotic desire possibly have to do with their great public undertaking? There are a few obvious answers. Petrarch's lyrics, most of them sonnets, were easily the most accomplished vernacular poems Europe had to show. If the sonnet had worked for Italian, perhaps it would work for Spanish, French, and English. The sonnet also had the advantage of being a courtly form, and the monarchic settings in which the new poets worked valued such expression. And despite its brevity, the sonnet demanded exquisite artfulness and thus provided welcome proof of the literary accomplishment for which the new poetry strove. And even the longing, the self-alienation, the idolatry that characterized the sonnet closely matched the idolatrous self-estrangement of empire itself. No wonder then that Petrarch's infatuation with Laura and his answering infatuation with Rome were echoed in the verse of his sixteenth-century followers. Like him, they found in the poetry of love a way of talking about the experiential side of the project of imperial self-making in which they were engaged.

Yet despite all that drew them toward the sonnet and the poetry of erotic desire, the new poets also discovered a tension between their imperial ambition and their devotion to love. The most poignant example of this tension is the very poem that has been the subject of this essay, Garcilaso's sonnet from Carthage with its dramatic shift from the triumphant Roman renewal of the opening quatrains to identification with Dido in the last few lines. But the fissure this poem discovers in the imperial project of arms and letters—a split between empire and love—opened repeatedly in the new poetry of sixteenth-century Europe, so frequently that it may be thought one of that poetry's most characteristic elements. Sidney wrote of almost nothing else, while Spenser, du Bellay, and Ronsard were in their different ways similarly divided.

And, finally, at least in its first generation in Spain, France, and England, the new poetry was intensely collaborative and was associated particularly with two leading poets, Boscán and Garcilaso, Ronsard and du Bellay, Sidney and Spenser. I say "in its first generation" because in the most fundamental sense of a "movement" poetry intent on remaking the vernacular through imitation, the new poetry went on for many generations. Indeed, though by then Petrarch, the sonnet, and the Italian dominance had wholly disappeared, one might say that eighteenth-century neoclassicism is a distant extension of the new poetry. Not until Romantic ideas of originality supplanted imitation as the basic mode of poetic invention could the new poetry be thought to have exhausted its founding impulse, and even then the newness of the new poetry continued to link it to the innovative literary movements of the nineteenth and twentieth centuries. In that regard, the new poetry of sixteenth-century Europe is as much an early modern as it is a Renaissance phenomenon. The new poets do, of course, look back. They take their models from ancient Greece and Rome and from more recent Renaissance Italy. But in their sense that a new poetry was needed, they were no less influenced by the newness of their age: the new technologies of print, artillery, and long-distance, compass-based navigation, the new monarchy, newly reformed religion (remember Cristóbal de Castillejo comparing Boscán and Garcilaso to Protestant heretics), the New World with its New Spain, New France, and New England, the new philosophy that "calls all in doubt," and the equally unsettling new geography.

Not all these forms of the early modern new had yet manifested themselves in 1535 when Garcilaso wrote his sonnet from Carthage. But enough had to make their influence felt on his poem. "Arms and the fury of Mars" meant something quite different in an age of artillery than it would have meant less than a century earlier. The new monarchy gave a more concrete political sense to the notion of restoring Rome. Print made the art of Italy and antiquity more readily available to both poets and their readers. The new geography strengthened identification with place. And new humanist education immersed young men like Garcilaso in a Latin culture where Virgil figured centrally and where even male friendship took on a new, more intense complexion. A poem of multifaceted literary recollection, Garcilaso's sonnet from Carthage is also a poem of a new world of invention, discovery, and feeling. In terms of the modernist definition of poetry, it is news that stays new, news of a newness that was in the sixteenth century radically transforming the world but news too of an undoing—a me deshago—that perennially opposes the triumphant march of renovative imperial conquest and expansion.

Part II
Garcilaso's Tunisian Poems
A BILINGUAL ANTHOLOGY

Translations by William Gahan and Richard Helgerson

The five poems that are here reprinted and translated were written in the fourteen months from October 1534 to the end of 1535. They thus all come from the period of the Tunis expedition itself (mid-June to mid-August 1535), the preparations that led up to it, and its immediate aftermath—all matters in which Garcilaso was directly engaged—and are, as such, the most proximate literary companions of the sonnet from Carthage that has been the subject of this essay.

In editions dating back to the sixteenth century and continuing down to the present, these poems will be found scattered according to their appropriate generic categories. The sonnet "A Mario" appears with Garcilaso's other sonnets, where it is normally numbered 35. (The sonnet from Carthage, which I do not reprint here, usually gets number 33, though chronologically it follows "A Mario.") In these standard editions, the elegies appear by themselves, following the sonnets and *canciones*, and are numbered elegy 1, for the one to the duke of Alba, and elegy 2, for the one to Boscán. Then comes the epistle to Boscán, Garcilaso's only verse epistle. And finally, after his three famous eclogues, one would find the three surviving Latin odes, of which the one to Ginés de Sepúlveda is normally identified as ode 3. To restore the immediacy of their original composition, I have abandoned this conventional distribution, dropped the conveniently familiar but anachronistic numberings, and printed the poems in the order in which they were most likely written. In that ordering, the sonnet from Carthage would follow the epistle to Boscán and the sonnet "A Mario" and precede the elegy to Boscán, the elegy to Alba, and the ode to Sepúlveda.

Despite the changes in ordering and numbering, I have retained generic labels as part of the title of each poem because, whatever other purposes these poems may have served, deliberate generic innovation was central to Garcilaso's intention for them. That is why they have from the first counted as significant additions to the new poetry of sixteenth-century Spain. The sonnet represents one of the two Italianate and especially Petrarchan genres—the other being the *canción*—that over the previous decade Garcilaso and Boscán had introduced into Spanish. In their generic self-consciousness, the other four poems are, if anything, even more deliberately innovative: the blank-verse epistle to Boscán is the first classical epistle in Spanish; the two elegies are the first two Spanish representatives of their kind; and the Latin ode is one of the first attempts by a Spanish poet to master this form in the language of antiquity.

The notes provide the bare minimum needed for comprehension and make no effort to replicate even a fraction of the vast commentary that has accumulated around these poems over the centuries. For the earliest annotations, see Antonio Gallego Morell, *Garcilaso de la Vega y sus comentaristas*. Elias Rivers's 1974 *Obras completas con comentario* includes an ample selection of both earlier and more recent commentary.

Epistle to Boscán

Señor Boscán, one who takes pleasure in relating his thoughts, even of things that have no name, will never be at a loss for matter with you, nor will need to seek out a ready style other than that pure ornament which befits a learned epistle. Among the very great benefits our perfect friendship grants us is this free and pure informality, far from affected weightiness; and thus, enjoying that liberty, I say I came with as sure a step as that with which I rode for twelve days, as you will only see as you make your way to the end of this letter.

I allow freer and looser rein to my fancy than to my horse, and it bears me at times over a path so sweet and pleasant that I forget past torments; at others, it carries me over passes so rough that the strain of the present ordeal makes me forget past ones; at times, I follow a pleasant mean, clear and restful, which takes my thoughts toward poetic invention and taste. One day, as I rode along considering the benefits of all who have, with outstretched hand, shown the way of friendship, and you, who exemplify friendship, at once came to mind; with you at least one great and apparently extraordinary thing happens to me: to tell you in a few lines, it is that, considering the benefits, honors, and pleasures that come to me from your friendship, which I hold so dear, I nevertheless count as still more valuable, nor does anything give me more sweet felicity, than the love I feel for you. This holds me so strongly that

---

Dated from Avignon October 12, 1534, this blank-verse Horatian epistle, the first of its kind in Spanish, would seem to have been composed as Garcilaso rode from Barcelona carrying a dispatch from Charles V to Don Pedro de Toledo, the emperor's viceroy in Naples.

the way of friendship: according to Herrera, this discussion of friendship draws on book 8 of Aristotle's *Nicomachean Ethics*

Epístola a Boscán

Señor Boscán, quien tanto gusto tiene
de daros cuenta de los pensamientos,
hasta las cosas que no tienen nombre,
no le podrá faltar con vos materia,
ni será menester buscar estilo   5
presto, distinto d'ornamento puro
tal qual a culta epístola conviene.
Entre muy grandes bienes que consigo
el amistad perfetta nos concede
es aqueste descuydo suelto y puro,   10
lexos de la curiosa pesadumbre;
y assí, d'aquesta libertad gozando,
digo que vine, quanto a lo primero,
tan sano como aquel que en doze días
lo que sólo veréys á caminado   15
quando el fin de la carta os lo mostrare.
Alargo y suelto a su plazer la rienda,
mucho más que al cavallo, al pensamiento,
y llévame a las vezes por camino
tan dulce y agradable que me haze   20
olvidar el trabajo del passado;
otras me lleva por tan duros passos
que con la fuerça del afán presente
también de los passados se me olvida;
a vezes sigo un agradable medio   25
honesto y reposado, en que'l discurso
del gusto y del ingenio se exercita.
Iva pensando y discurriendo un día
a quántos bienes alargó la mano
el que del amistad mostró el camino,   30
y luego vos, del amistad enxemplo,
os me ofrecéys en estos pensamientos,
y con vos a lo menos me acontece
una gran cosa, al parecer estraña,
y porque lo sepáys en pocos versos,   35
es que, considerando los provechos,
las honras y los gustos que me vienen
desta vuestra amistad, que en tanto tengo,
ninguna cosa en mayor precio estimo
ni me haze gustar del dulce estado   40

though well aware of the other aspects of our friendship and closeness, my soul is moved by this alone; and I know that here delight profits me as nowhere else, for it is usually put off for more useful and serious things. Continually seeing its forceful effect makes me examine its cause, and I discover that the benefit, distinction, joy, and pleasure that come to me from this loving tie with which our nature has bound our hearts are things that do not extend beyond myself, and in myself alone the benefit is made known. But love, from which fortunately all things are born, including any that might serve your use and pleasure, is itself reason enough for me to hold it in higher esteem than anything else, for how much more noble and virtuous it is to do good than to receive it; thus I delight in loving, and find that my delight is no folly.

O how ashamed and sorry I am to have praised the hospitality along the French road and its inns! Ashamed that you can now rightly take me for a liar; sorry to have wasted time praising a place that now merits only blame, where you will find only lies, sour wines, ugly waitresses, greedy servants, poor staging posts, high prices, little money, and a long road to arrive in Naples at last, without leaving any treasure buried there, unless you say that which can never be found nor had is buried. Give my lord

tanto como el amor de parte mía.
Éste comigo tiene tanta fuerça
que, sabiendo muy bien las otras partes
del amistad y la estrecheza nuestra,
con solo aquéste el alma se enternece;   45
y sé que otramente me aprovecha
el deleyte, que suele ser pospuesto
a las útiles cosas y a las graves.
Llévame a escudriñar la causa desto
ver contino tan rezio en mí el effetto,   50
y hallo que'l provecho, el ornamento,
el gusto y el plazer que se me sigue
del vínculo d'amor, que nuestro genio
enrredó sobre nuestros coraçones,
son cosas que de mí no salen fuera,   55
y en mí el provecho solo se convierte.
Mas el amor, de donde por ventura
naçen todas las cosas, si ay alguna,
que a vuestra utilidad y gusto miren,
es gran razón que ya en mayor estima   60
tenido sea de mí que todo el resto,
quanto más generosa y alta parte
es el hazer el bien que el recebille;
assí que amando me deleyto, y hallo
que no es locura este deleyte mío.   65
   ¡O quán corrido estoy y arrepentido
d'averos alabado el tratamiento
del camino de Francia y las posadas!
Corrido de que ya por mentiroso
con razón me ternéys; arrepentido   70
d'aver perdido tiempo en alabaros
cosa tan digna ya de vituperio,
donde no hallaréys sino mentiras,
vinos azedos, camareras feas,
barletes codiciosos, malas postas,   75
gran paga, poco argén, largo camino;
llegar al fin a Nápoles, no aviendo
dexado allá enterrado algún thesoro,
salvo si no dezís que's enterrado
lo que nunca se halla ni se tiene.   80
A mi señor Durall estrechamente

Durall a full embrace for me, if you can manage it. October twelfth, from the land where Petrarch's bright flame was born and from where the ashes of this fire remain.

---

my lord Durall: identified by Herrera as Mosén Dural, a wealthy and apparently fat knight in Barcelona

Petrarch's bright flame: Laura, whose tomb had been discovered a year earlier in Avignon

abraçá de mi parte, si pudierdes.
Doze del mes d'otubre, de la tierra
do nació el claro fuego del Petrarca
y donde están del fuego las cenizas.   85

Sonnet to Mario, being, as some say, wounded in the tongue and in the arm

Mario, this ungrateful love, as witness to my pure faith and my great steadfastness, exerting his vile nature in me by most harming him who is most his friend,

fearing that if I write and speak of his nature, I debase his grandeur, not content with his own efforts at cruelty, has strengthened my enemy's hand;

and thus, in the place that governs my right hand and in that which declares my soul's conceits, was I injured.

But I will make that offense dearly cost the offender, now that I am cured, free, desperate, and wronged.

This sonnet was written to Garcilaso's Neapolitan friend Mario Galeota sometime after the poet was wounded in the tongue and right arm in a skirmish outside the fortress of Goleta on June 22, 1535.

this ungrateful love: Cupid

Soneto a Mario, estando según algunos dizen, herido en la lengua y en el braço

Mario, el ingrato amor, como testigo
de mi fe pura y de mi gran firmeza,
usando en mí su vil naturaleza,
qu'es hazer más ofensa al más amigo,   4
    teniendo miedo que si escrivo y digo
su condición, abato su grandeza,
no bastando su esfuerço a su crüeza,
ha esforçado la mano a mi enemigo;   8
    y ansí, en la parte que la diestra mano
govierna y en aquella que declara
los concettos del alma, fuy herido.   11
    Mas yo haré que aquesta offensa cara
le cueste al offensor, ya que estoy sano,
libre, desesperado y offendido.   14

Elegy to Boscán

Here, Boscán, where Mantuan Virgil preserves the good Trojan Anchises' ashes with eternal name and life,
under the illustrious standard of Caesar Africanus, we find ourselves, the victors, gathered:
diverse in our purposes, some dying to harvest from our efforts the fruit that we sowed with sweat;
others (who make virtue the friend and prize of their labors and want people to think and say as much)
differ from the others in public, while in private God knows how much they contradict what they profess.
I take the middle way, for I never really cared to strive for wealth, and so I lift myself a little higher than them;
nor do I follow the narrow path of those who, I surely know, pull their reins toward the other path in the dark of night.
But where has my pen taken me? Step by step I slip into satire, and what I am writing you is an elegy.
I, sir, at last direct my steps where you know his destiny has always carried and carries Garcilaso;
and thus in the midst of this dense forest I sustain myself with its diversities, not without difficulty, but not for this
do I abandon the muses, but rather I pass back and forth between them and my duties, and thus variously occupied, I pleasantly enjoy myself in their company.
Thus the hours slip deceptively away; thus from harsh labor and heavy sorrow we take a stray hour's rest.
From here we shall go to see the land of the Siren, which clearly shows how full of leisure and love it was in ancient times.

This elegy, probably the first poem of this sort in Spanish, was written from Trapani in Sicily around late August of 1535, following Charles V's victorious return from his expedition in Tunis.

Anchises: the father of Aeneas whose burial is memorialized in Virgil's *Aeneid* 3.707-710

Caesar Africanus: Charles V, who, like the two Roman Scipios, was titled "Africanus" for his victory in North Africa

land of the Siren: Naples

Elegía a Boscán

Aquí, Boscán, donde del buen troyano
Anchises con eterno nombre y vida
conserva la ceniza el Mantüano,
   debaxo de la seña esclarecida
de Cæsar affricano nos hallamos   5
la vencedora gente recogida:
   diversos en estudio, que unos vamos
muriendo por coger de la fatiga
el fruto que con el sudor sembramos;
   otros (que hazen la virtud amiga   10
y premio de sus obras y assí quieren
que la gente lo piense y que lo diga)
   destotros en lo público difieren,
y en lo secreto sabe Dios en quánto
se contradizen en lo que profieren.   15
   Yo voy por medio, porque nunca tanto
quise obligarme a procurar hazienda,
que un poco más que aquéllos me levanto;
   ni voy tampoco por la estrecha senda
de los que cierto sé que a la otra vía   20
buelven, de noche al caminar, la rienda.
   Mas ¿dónde me llevó la pluma mía?,
que a sátira me voy mi passo a passo,
y aquesta que os escrivo es elegía.
   Yo endereço, señor, en fin mi passo   25
por donde vos sabéys que su processo
siempre á llevado y lleva Garcilasso;
   y assí, en mitad d'aqueste monte espesso,
de las diversidades me sostengo,
no sin dificultad, mas no por esso   30
   dexo las musas, antes torno y vengo
dellas al negociar, y varïando,
con ellas dulcemente me entretengo.
   Assí se van las oras engañando;
assí del duro afán y grave pena   35
estamos algún ora descansando.
   D'aquí iremos a ver de la Serena
la patria, que bien muestra aver ya sido
de ocio y d'amor antiguamente llena.

There my heart once had its nest, but, sadly, I do not know whether it is now occupied or destroyed;

from this a cold chill suddenly rushes through my bones in such a manner that I cannot bear it for a moment.

If, alas, I had been absent from my love only briefly, I do not deny that I would now live in greater security:

a brief absence has the same effect in love's smithy as a little water has on a fiery forge,

which you will see not only usually fails to put it out, but reinforces it with a more intense and burning flame;

this is because an opponent, faced with a slight challenge from its rival, to win the fight strengthens its arm and enforces its valor.

But if water in great quantity is scattered and poured over the fire, smoke mounts to the sky, noise is heard,

and the bright splendor of the lively flame, turned to dust and ashes, leaves little but its memory:

thus long absence has abundantly scattered its moisture, which extinguishes the fire love kept burning,

leaving it so that one's hand could touch it without peril in the moment when it noisily burns out.

I alone escape this rule, for love afflicts and torments me and in absence the misery I feel grows;

and I think that reason consents to and allows the cause of this exception which I alone among all experience

because by heavenly decree I have been eternally subject to and elected for the fire of love into which I enter,

thus, for it to be extinguished, absence must be without end, infinite, unlimited by time,

Allí mi coraçón tuvo su nido   40
un tiempo ya, mas no sé, triste, agora
o si estará ocupado o desparzido;
   d'aquesto un frio temor assí a desora
por mis huessos discurre en tal manera
que no puedo bivir con él un' ora.   45
   Si, triste, de mi bien yo estado uviera
un breve tiempo ausente, no lo niego
que con mayor seguridad biviera:
   la breve ausencia haze el mismo juego
en la fragua d'amor que en fragua ardiente   50
el agua moderada haze al fuego,
   la qual verás que no tan solamente
no le suele matar, mas le refuerça
con ardor más intenso y eminente,
   porque un contrario, con la poca fuerça   55
de su contrario, per vencer la lucha
su braço abiva y su valor esfuerça.
   Pero si el agua en abundancia mucha
sobre'l fuego s'esparze y se derrama,
el humo sube al cielo, el son s'escucha   60
   y, el claro resplandor de biva llama
en polvo y en ceniza convertido,
apenas queda dél sino la fama:
   assí el ausencia larga, que á esparzido
en abundancia su licor que amata   65
el fuego que'l amor tenia encendido,
   de tal suerte lo dexa que lo trata
la mano sin peligro en el momento
que en aparencia y son se desbarata.
   Yo solo fuera voy d'aqueste cuento,   70
porque'l amor m'aflige y m'atormenta
y en el ausencia crece el mal que siento;
   y pienso yo que la razón consienta
y permita la causa deste effeto,
que a mí solo entre todos se presenta,   75
   porque como del cielo yo sujeto
estava eternamente y diputado
al amoroso fuego en que me meto,
   assí, para poder ser amatado,
el ausencia sin término, infinita   80
deve ser, y sin tiempo limitado;

which reason will not allow, for the more and more absence lasts, it ends with life, which is finite.

But for me, who can assure me that my ill fortune will not conspire with change and forgetfulness against me?

This fear chases hope away and oppresses and weakens the great desire my eyes have of seeing their joy;

with them I now see only this sorrow that breaks my heart, and against it and myself I here struggle.

O harsh, o severe, o fierce Mars, covered with a diamond tunic and forever hardened in every part!

What can the tender lover do with your hardness and rough activity, always led on by fury?

By misfortune engaged in your business, I am reduced to such straits that death will be my final reward;

and my hard fate did not allow me to be suddenly run through with sharp and strong steel in battle,

so that I might waste away seeing my beloved and sweet fruit in the hands of another, and the cruel possessor mocking me.

But where does this sad fear transport me, estranging me from my own good sense? To a place filled with shame and sorrow,

where, if I saw the worst, my misery could not increase in the least, for in imagining it I am already lost.

So it seems to me now, yet if it came in its very form and figure, I would consider my present state the more favorable,

and would always be grateful to fortune for showing me of my suffering only the portrait that my fear and my sorrow paint.

lo qual no avrá razón que lo permita,
porque por más y más que ausencia dure,
con la vida s'acaba, que's finita.

    Mas a mí ¿quien avrá que m'assegure   85
que mi mala fortuna con mudança
y olvido contra mí no se conjure?

    Este temor persigue la esperança
y oprime y enflaquece el gran desseo
con que mis ojos van de su holgança;   90

    con ellos solamente agora veo
este dolor que'l coraçón me parte,
y con él y comigo aquí peleo.

    ¡O crudo, o riguroso, o fiero Marte,
de túnica cubierto de diamante   95
y endurecido siempre en toda parte!,

    ¿qué tiene que hazer el tierno amante
con tu dureza y áspero exercicio,
llevado siempre del furor delante?

    Exercitando por mi mal tu officio,   100
soy reduzido a términos que muerte
será mi postrimero beneficio;

    y ésta no permitió mi dura suerte
que me sobreviniesse peleando,
de hierro traspassado agudo y fuerte,   105

    porque me consumiesse contemplando
mi amado y dulce fruto en mano agena,
y el duro possessor de mí burlando.

    Mas ¿dónde me trasporta y enagena
de mi propio sentido el triste miedo?   110
A parte de vergüença y dolor llena,

    donde, si el mal yo viesse, ya no puedo,
según con esperalle estoy perdido,
acrecentar en la miseria un dedo.

    Assí lo pienso agora, y si él venido   115
fuesse en su misma forma y su figura,
ternia el presente por mejor partido,

    y agradeceria siempre a la ventura
mostrarme de mi mal solo el retrato
que pintan mi temor y mi tristura.   120

I know what it is to place hope in self-delusion and to deal and converse only with it,

as happens to the wretched dying man who while, on one side, his true and sober friend shows him the seriousness of his condition,

and urges him to begin raising from his human body his unfettered soul to a better place with airy flight;

his tender wife, on the other side, unable to surrender to despair, hides from him the worst of his ill;

he, in the embrace of this sweet deception, turns his eyes to her kind voice and rejoices, to his soul's damage, as he dies:

so I turn my eyes from everything and set them only on the thought of hope, whether true or false;

in this sweet error I die happily, for seeing clearly and knowing my true state can no longer relieve the sorrow I feel,

and I end like one who in a warm bath dies without feeling it, having gently opened his own veins.

You, in your native land, among those who love you well, looking at the delightful shore and hearing the sound of the sea that breaks on it

and gazing without hindrance upon her to whom you are granting eternal fame in your lively writings,

rejoice, for a more beautiful flame than that which the burning of Troy made inflames your heart;

you have no need to fear the contrary movement of fortune, for a pure splendor calms the wind.

I, like a driven mercenary, go unwillingly wherever fortune directs me, except to die, which I do willingly;

only a delusion so weak that it must be renewed each day sustains my hope,

---

You: Boscán

in your native land: the region of Barcelona

    Yo sé qué cosa es esperar un rato
el bien del propio engaño y solamente
tener con él inteligencia y trato,
    como acontece al mísero doliente
que, del un cabo, el cierto amigo y sano   125
le muestra el grave mal de su acidente,
    y le amonesta que del cuerpo humano
comience a levantar a mejor parte
el alma suelta con bolar liviano;
    mas la tierna muger, de la otra parte,   130
no se puede entregar al desengaño
y encúbrele del mal la mayor parte;
    él abraçado con su dulce engaño,
buelve los ojos a la boz piadosa
y alégrase muriendo con su daño: 135
    assí los quito yo de toda cosa
y póngolos en solo el pensamiento
de la esperança, cierta o mentirosa ;
    en este dulce error muero contento,
porque ver claro y conocer mi 'stado   140
no puede ya curar el mal que siento,
    y acabo como aquel que'n un templado
baño metido, sin sentillo muere,
las venas dulcemente desatado.
    Tú, que en la patria, entre quien bien te quiere,   145
la deleytosa playa estás mirando
y oyendo el son del mar que en ella hiere,
    y sin impedimiento contemplando
la misma a quien tú vas eterna fama
en tus bivos escritos procurando,   150
    alégrate, que más hermosa llama
que aquella que'l troyano encendimiento
pudo causar, el coraçón t'inflama;
    no tienes que temer el movimiento
de la fortuna con soplar contrario,   155
que el puro resplandor serena el viento.
    Yo, como conduzido mercenario,
voy do fortuna a mi pesar m'embía,
si no a morir, quo aquéste's voluntario;
    solo sostiene la esperança mía   160
un tan débil engaño que de nuevo
es menester hazelle cada día,

and if I do not build and renew it, my hope falls to the ground so heavily that in vain I try to lift it.

This is the prize for my service, that only in my life's misery has fortune denied its usual fickleness.

Where can I flee so that the heavy charge that oppresses my weakened neck might be briefly shaken off?

But, o, distance does not unburden the sad heart, and misfortune, wherever I am, stretches out its arm to reach me:

whether where the fiery sun blazes in sandy Libya, the birthplace of all things poisonous and fierce,

or where it is forever overcome by frozen snow and cold wind, a place where no one lives or dwells,

if either to the former or to the latter madness or fortune were one day to take me and I were to waste there my whole life,

jealous fear with a cold hand would in the midst of heat and burning sand seize my sad heart;

and in the harshness of the ice, on a serene night, the wind blowing so sharp and pure it slows the water's swift flow,

from this living fire in which I am purified and hope to be consumed little by little, I know that even there I will not be safe, and thus torn between extremes I die.

y si no le fabrico y le renuevo,
da consigo en el suelo mi esperança
tanto que'n vano a levantalla pruevo.   165
    Aqueste premio mi servir alcança,
que en sola la miseria de mi vida
negó fortuna su común mudança.
    ¿Dónde podré hüir que sacudida
un rato sea de mí la grave carga   170
que oprime mi cerviz enflaquecida?
    Mas ¡ay!, que la distancia no descarga
el triste coraçón, y el mal, doquiera
que 'stoy, para alcançarme el braço alarga:
    si donde'l sol ardiente reverbera   175
en la arenosa Libya, engendradora
de toda cosa ponçoñosa y fiera,
    o adonde'l es vencido a qualquier ora
de la rígida nieve y viento frío,
parte do no so bive ni se mora,   180
    si en ésta o en aquélla el desvarío
o la fortuna me llevasse un día
y allí gastasse todo el tiempo mío,
    el çeloso temor con mano fría
en medio del calor y ardiente arena   185
el triste coraçón m'apretaría;
    y en el rigor del yelo, en la serena
noche, soplando el viento agudo y puro
que'l veloce correr del agua enfrena,
    d'aqueste bivo fuego, en que m'apuro   190
y consumirme poco a poco espero,
sé que aun allí no podré estar seguro,
y assí diverso entre contrarios muero.

Elegy to the Duke of Alba
on the Death of His Brother, Don Bernardino de Toledo

Though this heavy occasion has touched my soul with such emotion
that I need consolation
   to lighten the burden of my thought and end the force of my continuous weeping,
   I nevertheless wanted to test whether I had sufficient imagination to
write you something consoling, despite the state I am in, that might
serve
   to lessen the fury of your recent grief, if the muses can uplift a heavy
heart
   and put an end to your plaints, at which the inhabitants of Pindhos already show hurt and confusion;
   for as far as I know, neither when the sun shines, nor when it hides in
the sea, does your tearful state improve,
   rather, you remain this way wherever you are, your eyes always
drenched, and your weeping so responds to your sorrow
   that I fear to see your flesh and blood dissolved in tears, as mountain
snow is melted by wind-tossed rain.
   If perchance, from grieving anew with added energy, your troubled
thoughts become drowsy in common repose,
   in that brief dream a pallid image of the brother who departs from
sweet life appears,
   then you, reaching out your piteous hand, attempting to lift the
beloved body, lift only empty air;
   and from sorrow the dream being broken, you anxiously seek him out
who, with the dream, has already departed far away

This funeral elegy, which draws heavily on several Neo-Latin poems, including
particularly one by Gerolamo Fracastoro, was written between late August and
late October of 1535 and commemorates the death on the return from the Tunis expedition of Don Bernardino de Toledo, the younger brother of the duke
of Alba.

Elegía al duque d'Alva
en la muerte de don Bernaldino de Toledo

   Aunque'ste grave caso aya tocado
con tanto sentimiento el alma mía
que de consuelo estoy necessitado,
   con que de su dolor mi fantasía
se descargasse un poco y s'acabasse   5
de mi continuo llanto la porfía,
   quise, pero, provar si me bastasse
el ingenio a escrivirte algún consuelo,
estando qual estoy, que aprovechasse
   para que tu reziente desconsuelo   10
la furia mitigasse, si las musas
pueden un coraçón alçar del suelo
   y poner fin a las querellas que usas,
con que de Pindo ya las moradoras
se muestran lastimadas y confusas;   15
   que según é sabido, ni a las oras
que'l sol se muestra ni en el mar s'asconde,
de tu lloroso estado no mejoras,
   antes, en él permaneciendo donde—
quiera que estás, tus ojos siempre bañas,   20
y el llanto a tu dolor assí responde
   que temo ver deshechas tus entrañas
en lágrimas, como al lluvioso viento
se derrite la nieve en las montañas.
   Si acaso el trabajado pensamiento   25
en el común reposo s'adormeçe,
por tornar al dolor con nuevo aliento,
   en aquel breve sueño t'aparece
la imagen amarilla del hermano
que de la dulce vida desfallece,   30
   y tú tendiendo la piadosa mano,
provando a levantar el cuerpo amado,
levantas solamente el ayre vano,
   y del dolor el sueño desterrado,
con ansia vas buscando el que partido   35
era ya con el sueño y alongado.

Thus taking leave of your senses, as if beside yourself, along the river-banks of Trapani, with cries and wails,

you seek your beloved brother, who alone was half your soul, and who, by dying, has now left you as a broken part;

and you repeat the beloved name, with a disheveled appearance, turning on every side,

as near the Eridanus, plaintive Lampetia wept and cried out his name in vain, saddened by her brother's death:

"Waves, return my sweet brother Phaeton to me; if not, here you will see me die, watering this plain with my tears!"

O how many times, her strength revived by powerful suffering, did she renew her moans against her cruel and harsh fate;

and how many times besides, when that fury ended, would she, on the shady riverside, lifeless, weary, recline her body!

Truly I confess to you that if anything can sadden a noble soul among humans and mortals,

it may well be this one, for one blow has deprived you not only of a brother, but also of so sweet a friend;

who was not only a witness to your counsel and intimate secrets, but was as true to you as you are to yourself:

in him, your own judicious and sincere views resided, and the place from which they came could be seen in their effects;

in him, one by one, your graces and virtues could already be seen and discerned, and they shone with a beautiful light,

like a shining crystal column which is not shadowed by anything that approaches its living purity.

O miserable fates, o malicious fortune of this harsh human life, through which we suffer so many ordeals along the way,

---

Trapani: the Sicilian port where the Spanish troops disembarked

Eridanus: the river where Phaeton fell after losing control of his father Helios's horses

Lampetia: Phaeton's sister who in her grief at her brother's death was metamorphosed into a poplar tree

Assí desfalleciendo en tu sentido,
como fuera de ti, por la ribera
de Trápana con llanto y con gemido
   el charo hermano buscas, que solo era   40
la mitad de tu alma, el qual muriendo,
no quedará de ti ya parte entera;
   y no de otra manera repitiendo
vas el amado nombre, en desusada
figura a todas partes rebolviendo,   45
   que cerca del Erídano aquexada
lloró y llamó Lampetia el nombre en vano,
con la fraterna muerte lastimada:
   "¡Ondas, tornáme ya mi dulce hermano
Phætón; si no, aquí veréys mi muerte,   50
regando con mis ojos este llano!"
   ¡O quántas vezes, con el dolor fuerte
abivadas las fuerças, renovava
las quexas de su cruda y dura suerte;
   y quántas otras, quando s'acabava   55
aquel furor, en la ribera umbrosa,
muerta, cansada, el cuerpo reclinava!
   Bien te confiesso que s'alguna cosa
entre la humana puede y mortal gente
entristecer un alma generosa,   60
   con gran razón podrá ser la presente,
pues te á privado d'un tan dulce amigo,
no solamente hermano, un acidente;
   el qual no sólo siempre fue testigo
de tus consejos y íntimos secretos,   65
mas de quanto lo fuiste tú contigo:
   en él se reclinavan tus discretos
y honestos pareceres y hazían
conformes al asiento sus effettos;
   en él ya se mostravan y leýan   70
tus gracias y virtudes una a una
y con hermosa luz resplandecían,
   como en luziente de cristal coluna
que no encubre, de quanto s'avezina
a su biva pureza, cosa alguna.   75
   ¡O miserables hados, o mezquina
suerte, la del estado humano, y dura,
do por tantos trabajos se camina,

and now in this age, the evils are much greater, when the progress of misfortune moves from one ill to the next!

Which one of us by the great excess of wars, of dangers and exile, has not been affected and wearied?

Who has not seen his own blood spill from his enemy's steel? Who has not seen his life lost a thousand times before being saved by mistake?

How many have lost or will lose home, wife, and memory, and how many others will see their estate wasted!

What is gained by this? Some glory? Some prizes or gratitude? He who reads our story will know:

it will be clear that like dust in the wind, so will our arduous endeavor dissolve before whoever attempts to uphold it.

Not content with this, the enemy of humankind, who enviously steals the unripe grain from its stalk,

has willed to treat us so harshly that neither your youth, don Bernardino, nor our loss has made it merciful.

Who could have foreseen this? Who would not have been deceived by hope, seeing you walk along such a path?

Who would not have assured themselves of the complete safety of your youth, without fearing such a change in nature?

Not yours, but our own injuries should bring us sorrow, for bitter death clearly exposes our many illusions:

it has shown us already that in our long life we can hardly bear the heavy burden of our torments and troubles;

it has shown us through you that bright eyes, youth, grace, and beauty are also, when it wishes, its spoils.

But it cannot from your face, once deprived of life, hide the handiwork of nature:

y agora muy mayor la desventura
d'aquesta nuestra edad, cuyo progresso   80
muda d'un mal en otro su figura!
    ¿A quién ya de nosotros el ecesso
de guerras, de peligros y destierro
no toca y no á cansado el gran processo?
    ¿Quién no vio desparzir su sangre al hierro   85
del enemigo? ¿Quién no vio su vida
perder mil vezes y escapar por yerro?
    ¡De quántos queda y quedará perdida
la casa, la muger y la memoria,
y d'otros la hazienda despendida!   90
    ¿Qué se saca d'aquesto? ¿Alguna gloria?
¿Algunos premios o agradecimiento?
Sabrálo quien leyere nuestra historia:
    verásse allí que como polvo al viento,
assí se deshará nuestra fatiga   95
ante quien s'endereça nuestro intento.
    No contenta con esto, la enemiga
del humano linage, que embidiosa
coge sin tiempo el grano de la espiga,
    nos á querido ser tan rigurosa   100
que ni a tu juventud, don Bernaldino,
ni á sido a nuestra pérdida piadosa.
    ¿Quién pudiera de tal ser adevino?
¿A quién no le engañara la esperança,
viéndote caminar por tal camino?   105
    ¿Quién no se prometiera en abastança
seguridad entera de tus años,
sin temer de natura tal mudança?
    Nunca los tuyos, mas los propios daños
dolernos deven, que la muerte amarga   110
nos muestra claros ya mil desengaños:
    ános mostrado ya que en vida larga,
apenas de tormentos y d'enojos
llevar podemos la pesada carga;
    ános mostrado en ti que claros ojos   115
y juventud y gracia y hermosura
son también, quando quiere, sus despojos.
    Mas no puede hazer que tu figura,
despúes de ser de vida ya privada,
no muestre el arteficio de natura: 120

though to be sure, it is no longer imbued with the color of rose that once mixed with its lily white,

because the warmth that ignited the white snow of your pure face has already been robbed by death;

in all else, as if in a safe and restful dream you slept, giving promise of life to come.

But what will your mother do, whom you loved so much and by whom you were so madly loved, to whom you gave life with your life?

The sound of her cry, whose force cuts through the near and distant air, seems to me to have arrived even here,

and the cry of your four sisters follows so strongly that it contends in sheer force with that of your mother;

I observe them all tearing the fine gold from their long tresses, which they rend and abuse.

Old Tormes, with his chorus of lovely white nymphs, dries the river and soaks the ground with his crying,

not reclined over his urn in the sweet cool of his shadowy cavern, but instead sprawled on the sand in the scorching summer;

with rough cries and moans, he tears his unkempt hair, beard, and fine attire;

all around him his dismayed nymphs are crying, strewn on the ground without finery, their golden hair in disarray.

Cease now from suffering this pain, beautiful denizens of the deep Tormes; attempt something more helpful:

console the mother, for piteous sorrow has put her in such a state that urgent rescue is necessary.

Soon the body, entombed in perpetual marble, may be bathed in the waves of your Tormes;

Tormes: river that runs through the Alba estates in Castile

    bien es verdad que no está acompañada
de la color de rosa que solía
con la blanca açucena ser mezclada.

    porque'l calor templado que encendía
la blanca nieve de tu rostro puro,   125
robado ya la muerte te lo avía;

    en todo lo demás, como en seguro
y reposado sueño descansavas,
indicio dando del bivir futuro.

    Mas ¿qué hará la madre que tú amavas,   130
de quien perdidamente eras amado,
a quien la vida con la tuya davas?

    Aquí se me figura que á llegado
de su lamento el son, que con su fuerça
rompe el ayre vezino y apartado,   135

    tras el qual a venir también se 'sfuerça
el de las quatro hermanas, que teniendo
va con el de la madre a biva fuerça;

    a todas las contemplo desparziendo
de su cabello luengo el fino oro,   140
al qual ultraje y daño están haziendo.

    El viejo Tormes, con el blanco choro
de sus hermosas nymphas, seca el río
y humedece la tierra con su lloro,

    no recostado en urna al dulce frío   145
de su caverna umbrosa, mas tendido
por el arena en el ardiente estío;

    con ronco son de llanto y de gemido,
los cabellos y barvas mal paradas
se despedaça y el sotil vestido;   150

    en torno dél sus nymphas desmayadas
llorando en tierra están, sin ornamento,
con las cabeças d'oro despeynadas.

    Cesse ya del dolor el sentimiento,
hermosas moradoras del undoso   155
Tormes; tened más provechoso intento:

    consolad a la madre, que el piadoso
dolor la tiene puesta en tal estado
que es menester socorro presuroso.

    Presto será que'l cuerpo, sepultado   160
en un perpetuo mármol, de las ondas
podrá de vuestro Tormes ser bañado;

and you, beautiful chorus, who in the deep waters lie, perhaps you will be moved to answer my cry of pain.

You, elevated promontories, who meanwhile are saddened along with all Trinacria, seek relief from so much sorrow.

Satyrs, fauns, nymphs, whose lives pass without trouble, denizens of hidden and remote parts,

seek out, with your long experience and knowledge, herbs and flowers of occult properties to console Fernando:

thus in the hidden forest, when burning with vital and pleasing fire you pursue fleeting nymphs,

may they submit to your pitiable pleas, and, linked in reciprocal bonds, not avoid your amorous play.

You, great Fernando, who shine brightly in the midst of your past and present deeds, which must rise to even greater fame for having been yours,

take stock of yourself, for if you fall short of the name you have won among the people, your virtue is in someway weakened,

because a strong man may not face the accidents of Fortune with anything but a firm countenance and a brave heart:

and not only should this ill fortune, in its cruel and rigorous progress, with the turning of the sun, the heavens, and the moon,

never move a noble soul nor sadden it with mournful transport, disturbing its repose with cares;

but if the machinery of the heavens themselves, with a frightening sound and riotous noise, should be reduced to pieces and fall to earth,

your soul ought to be crushed by the heavy weight and reduced to shambles from this ruin before it is made fearful and distressed.

By these rough roads we travel to the lofty seat of immortality, where no one who strays from them ever arrives.

Trinacria: Sicily
Fernando: the duke of Alba

y tú, hermoso choro, allá en las hondas
aguas metido, podrá ser que al llanto
de mi dolor te muevas y respondas.   165
   Vos, altos promontorios, entretanto,
con toda la Trinacria entristecida,
buscad alivio en desconsuelo tanto.
   Sátyros, phaunos, nymphas, cuya vida
sin enojo se passa, moradores   170
de la parte repuesta y escondida,
   con luenga esperïencia sabidores,
buscad para consuelo de Fernando
yervas de propriedad oculta y flores:
   assí en el ascondido bosque, quando   175
ardiendo en bivo y agradable fuego
las fugitivas nymphas vays buscando,
   ellas se inclinen al piadoso ruego
y en recíproco lazo estén ligadas,
sin esquivar el amoroso juego.   180
   Tú, gran Fernando, que entre tus passadas
y tus presentes obras resplandeces,
y a mayor fama están por ti obligadas,
   contempla dónde 'stás, que si falleces
al nombre que as ganado entre la gente,   185
de tu virtud en algo t'enflaqueçes,
   porque al fuerte varón no se consiente
no resistir los casos de Fortuna
con firme rostro y coraçón valiente;
   y no tan solamente esta importuna,   190
con processo crüel y riguroso,
con rebolver de sol, de cielo y luna,
   mover no deve un pecho generoso
ni entristecello con funesto buelo,
turbando con molestia su reposo,   195
   mas si toda la máchina del cielo
con espantable son y con rüydo,
hecha pedaços, se viniere al suelo,
   deve ser aterrado y oprimido
del grave peso y de la gran rüyna   200
primero que espantado y comovido.
   Por estas asperezas se camina
de la inmortalidad al alto asiento,
do nunca arriba quien d'aquí declina.

And after all, sir, in considering human nature, I concede to our weaker side some sentiment,

but its excesses in this, insofar as I can, I forbid and restrain, if it appears intent on persisting without end.

At least time, which reduces and changes the state of all things, should be enough if reason fails:

the Trojan prince was not forever mourned by his distraught father, nor was he forever grieved by his mother;

rather, after the body was ransomed with humble tears and with gold, and relinquished by fierce Achilles,

repressing the lamentable chorus of their Phrygian wail, they put an end to their vain and profitless emotion and weeping.

The tender heart of Venus, human in this, what did it feel, seeing her Adonis soak the green plain with his blood?

But once she clearly saw, her eyes bleary with tears, that she did nothing with her weeping but undo herself,

and that her crying could not bring back her beloved and sweet friend from dark and gloomy night to the light of day,

she washed her eyes and somewhat more contentedly showed forth her pure brow, leaving sorrow with her dead lover.

And then with graceful steps she moved over the green ground, in her accustomed garland and finery;

in wanton flight the wind loosened her hair, and her gaze gladdened earth, sea, and sky.

With discourse and reason, which foresees so much, with fortitude and being, which I observe in you, may weak sadness be spurned.

Your burning desire to climb the temple where death loses its supremacy is enough for you, without my showing you another example;

---

the Trojan prince: Hector, killed by Achilles

Y en fin, señor, tornando al movimiento   205
de la humana natura, bien permito
a nuestra flaca parte un sentimiento,
   mas el ecesso en esto vedo y quito,
si alguna cosa puedo, que parece
que quiere proceder en infinito.   210
   A lo menos el tiempo, que descrece
y muda de las cosas el estado,
deve bastar, si la razón fallece:
   no fue el troyano príncipe llorado
siempre del viejo padre dolorido,   215
ni siempre de la madre lamentado;
   antes, después del cuerpo redemido
con lágrimas umildes y con oro,
que fue del fiero Achilles concedido,
   y reprimiendo el lamentable choro   220
del frigio llanto, dieron fin al vano
y sin provecho sentimiento y lloro.
   El tierno pecho, en esta parte humano,
de Venus, ¿qué sintió, su Adonis viendo
de su sangre regar el verde llano?   225
   Mas desque vido bien que, corrompiendo
con lágrimas sus ojos, no hazía
sino en su llanto estarse deshaziendo,
   y que tornar llorando no podía
su charo y dulce amigo de la escura   230
y tenebrosa noche al claro día,
   los ojos enxugó y la frente pura
mostró con algo más contentamiento,
dexando con el muerto la tristura.
   Y luego con gracioso movimiento   235
se fue su passo por el verde suelo,
con su guirlanda usada y su ornamento;
   desordenava con lascivo buelo
el viento sus cabellos; con su vista
s'alegrava la tierra, el mar y el cielo.   240
   Con discurso y razón, que's tan prevista,
con fortaleza y ser, que en ti contemplo,
a la flaca tristeza se resista.
   Tu ardiente gana de subir al templo
donde la muerte pierde su derecho   245
te basta, sin mostrarte yo otro enxemplo;

there you will see how little damage death has done to the memory and bright glory of the famous men it has undone.

Turn your eyes where in the end supreme hope beckons you, where the soul ascends, perfected and purged in a pure flame;

do you think it was a different fire that consumed the mortal part of Alcides in Oeta, while his spirit flew to the lofty prize?

In this way, he for whom your heart scatters a thousand sighs a day, and for whom your cries everywhere resound,

ascended through the difficult and lofty passage, purged and purified of his mortal flesh, to the sweet region of joy,

where with free reason and in safety he observes the vanity of mortals, blind men, wanderers in the dark air,

and seeing and considering our misfortunes, is gladdened to have taken flight and happy to enjoy immortal hours.

He stands upon the immense and crystalline sky, with at each hand his bright father and his sublime grandfather:

The one sees in his human descendants the presence of his own virtues, which made the rough road smooth;

the other, who here remained less among men in mortal life, displays there his glorious wounds.

(Through these the prize is won there, for in heaven it is not fitting to exact from the enemy any other revenge.)

He considers the earth and the sea that contains it, holding and judging it all as a small speck next to heaven;

his gaze fixed upon that great record and mirror where the past with the future and the present is joined,

he looks upon the duration of your life, which is limited from on high, Fernando, and he sees your place already decreed.

Alcides: Hercules, whose body was consumed on a funeral pyre on Mount Oeta

his bright father: Don García de Toledo, who died young in battle

his sublime grandfather: Don Fadrique de Toledo

allí verás quán poco mal á hecho
la muerte en la memoria y clara fama
de los famosos hombres que á deshecho.
    Buelve los ojos donde al fin te llama   250
la suprema esperança, do perfeta
sube y purgada el alma en pura llama;
    ¿piensas que es otro el fuego que en Oeta
d'Alcides consumió la mortal parte
quando boló el espirtu a la alta meta?   255
    Desta manera aquél, por quien reparte
tu coraçón sospiros mil al día
y resuena tu llanto en cada parte,
    subió por la difícil y alta vía,
de la carne mortal purgado y puro,   260
en la dulce región del alegría,
    do con discurso libre ya y seguro
mira la vanidad de los mortales,
ciegos, errados en el ayre 'scuro,
    y viendo y contemplando nuestros males,   265
alégrase d'aver alçado el buelo
y gozar de las oras immortales.
    Pisa el immenso y cristalino cielo,
teniendo puestos d'una y d'otra mano
el claro padre y el sublime agüelo: 270
    el uno ve de su processo humano
sus virtudes estar allí presentes,
que'l áspero camino hazen llano;
    el otro, que acá hizo entre las gentes
en la vida mortal menor tardança,   275
sus llagas muestra allá resplandecientes.
    (Dellas aqueste premio allá s'alcança,
porque del enemigo no conviene
procurar en el cielo otra vengança.)
    Mira la tierra, el mar que la contiene,   280
todo lo qual por un pequeño punto
a respetto del cielo juzga y tiene;
    puesta la vista en aquel gran trassunto
y espejo do se muestra lo passado
con lo futuro y lo presente junto,   285
    el tiempo que a tu vida limitado
d'allá 'riba t'está, Fernando, mira,
y allí ve tu lugar ya deputado.

O fortunate one, who without anger, without hate, are in peace, without blind love, for which here we die and pine after;

in eternal pleasure and peace, you live and will live for as long as souls are inflamed by the fire of divine love!

And if merciful and generous heaven gives long life to the voice of my lamentation, which you know it aims for and desires,

I promise you, friend, that while the sun gives light to the world and the dark night covers the earth with its mantle,

for as long as fish inhabit moist depths of the sea and fierce beasts dwell in dense forests,

you will be sung all the world over, for no matter how much it is debated, there will never be seen another of your age to equal you, from the Antarctic to Callisto.

Callisto: the Great Bear, the constellation associated with the North Pole

¡O bienaventurado, que sin ira,
sin odio, en paz estás, sin amor ciego,   290
con quien acá se muere y se sospira,
   y en eterna holgança y en sosiego
bives y bivirás quanto encendiere
las almas del divino amor el fuego!
   Y si el cielo piadoso y largo diere   295
luenga vida a la boz deste mi llanto,
lo qual tú sabes que pretiende y quiere,
   yo te prometo, amigo, que entretanto
que el sol al mundo alumbre y que la escura
noche cubra la tierra con su manto,   300
   y en tanto que los peces la hondura
húmida habitarán del mar profundo
y las fieras del monte la espessura,
   se cantará de ti por todo el mundo,
que en quanto se discurre, nunca visto   305
de tus años jamás otro segundo
será, desdel Antártico a Calisto.

Ode to Ginés de Sepúlveda

Since the power to draw the bow of religion and of fierce war back farther to such an extent that its curved ends meet without resistance

the muse has granted to you alone, learned Sepúlveda, in a similar manner it falls to you also to tell of fearful Africa under an intrepid and pious king,

who mounted on his famous pied stallion, moves rapidly through the tight ranks, outrunning the swift wind, fervent as he brandishes the death-dealing lance in his hand;

to whom the rabble yields just as the light stubble gives way to flames in a dry grove or clouds to shifting winds in the open sky.

While he impetuously assaults the timorous with constant turning, as the fierce lion through Massylian or Numidian forests harries peaceful beasts,

the wives, recently bereft of their lovers, sigh with a trembling breast, accustomed to gaze from the high towers over the wide plains of the field.

"O, young men," they cry, "avoid with your unequal strength the arms of Caesar and their abominable encounters. When to posterity

his sacrificed mother gave his name, as they struggled to pull the weak infant from her womb, from this proceeds the Caesarean race, from this the delight in new slaughter: Do you think

---

Written to the Spanish humanist Juan Ginés de Sepúlveda in the last months of 1535 or the first months of 1536, this Latin ode draws on Horace's *Odes* 3.2 and on phrases from book 12 of Virgil's *Aeneid*.

to draw the bow of religion: alludes to Sepúlveda's *Democrites*, which argues for the legitimacy of Christian warfare

to tell of fearful Africa: Sepúlveda had been commissioned to write a history of the Tunis expedition an intrepid and pious king: Charles V

Caesar: Charles V

his sacrificed mother: the mother of Julius Caesar, who died giving birth by caesarean section

Ode ad Genesium Sepulvedam

Arcum quando adeo relligionis et
saevae militiae ducere longius,
   ut curvata coire
     inter se capita haud negent,   4

uni musa tibi, docte Sepulveda,
concessit: pariter dicere et Africam
   incumbit pavitantem
     sub rege intrepido et pio,   8

qui insigni maculis vectus equo citos
praevertit rapidus densa per agmina
   ventos, fervidus hastam
     laetalem quatiens manu;   12

dat cui non aliter turba locum leves
quam flammis stipulae per nemus aridum
   aut coelum per apertum
     ventis dant nebulae vagis.   16

Pugnax perpetuo dum trepidos agit
giro, saevus uti Massylias leo
   per sylvas Nomadasve
     imbelles agitat feras,   20

suspirant timido pectore, turribus
ex altis aciem lata per aequora
   campi tendere suetae,
     sponsae nuper amoribus   24

orbatae: "Heu, iuvenes, Caesaris," inquiunt,
"vitate imparibus viribus armaque
   congressusque nefandos.
     Quando nomina posteris   28

mater caesa dedit, dum puerum student
languentem eruere e visceribus, genus
   hinc est caesareum, hinc est
     gaudens caede nova: putas   32

that he who from a funereal threshold thrust his savage foot into life would not derive from this and engender in others a native fury and a thirst for hot blood?"

saevum funereo limine qui pedem
ad vitam imposuit, non ferat indidem
    ingeneretque furorem
        et caedis calidae sitim?"

Bibliography

Editions and Translations

Ariosto, Ludovico. *Cinque Canti / Five Cantos.* Ed. and trans. Alexander Sheers and David Quint. Biblioteca Italiana. Berkeley: University of California Press, 1996.

———. *Orlando furioso.* Trans. Barbara Reynolds. 2 vols. Harmondsworth, Middlesex: Penguin Books, 1975.

Ascham, Roger. *The Scholemaster.* Ed. R. J. Schoeck. Don Mills, Ontario: J. M. Dent, 1966.

Bembo, Pietro. *Prose della volgar lingua.* Ed. Mario Marti. Padua: Liviana Editrice, 1967.

Boscán, Juan. *Obras.* Ed. Carlos Clavería. Barcelona: PPU, 1991.

Bruno, Giordano. *The Heroic Frenzies.* Trans. Paul Eugene Memmo. Chapel Hill: University of North Carolina Press, 1964.

Camões, Luís de. *The Lusiads.* Trans. William C. Atkinson. 1952. Reprint, Harmondsworth, Middlesex: Penguin Books, 1973.

———. *The Lusíads.* Trans. Landeg White. Oxford: Oxford University Press, 1997.

———. *Selected Sonnets: A Bilingual Edition.* Trans. William Baer. Chicago: University of Chicago Press, 2005.

Castiglione, Baldesar. *The Book of the Courtier: The Singleton Translation.* Ed. Daniel Javitch. New York: W. W. Norton, 2002.

Castillejo, Cristóbal de. *Obras.* Ed. J. Domínguez Bordona. Madrid: Espasa-Calpe, 1944.

Cervantes, Miguel de. *Don Quijote de la Mancha.* Ed. Martin de Riquer. Barcelona: Editorial Planeta, 1992.

Charles V. *Correspondenz des Kaisers Karl V.* Ed. Karl Lans. 3 vols. Frankfurt: Minerva, 1966.

Daniel, Samuel. *Poems and "A Defence of Ryme."* Ed. Arthur Colby Sprague. 1930. Reprint, Chicago: University of Chicago Press, 1965.

Du Bellay, Joachim. *Œuvres poétiques.* Ed. Daniel Aris and Françoise Joukovsky. 2 vols. Paris: Classiques Garnier, 1993.

———. *"The Regrets" with "The Antiquities of Rome," Three Latin Elegies, and "The Defense and Enrichment of the French Language."* Ed. and trans. Richard Helgerson. Philadelphia: University of Pennsylvania Press, 2006.

Garcilaso de la Vega. *Garcilaso de la Vega y sus comentaristas.* Ed. Antonio Gallego Morell. 2nd ed. Madrid: Editorial Gredos, 1972.

———. *Obras completas con comentario.* Ed. Elias L. Rivers. Madrid: Editorial Castalia, 1974.

———. *Obras Completas.* Ed. Amancio Labandeira. Madrid: Fundación Universitaria Española, 1981.

———. *Obras de Garcilaso del la Vega con anotaciones de Fernando de Herrera.* Seville: A. de la Barrera, 1580.

———. *Poesías Castellanas Completas.* Ed. Elias L. Rivers. 3rd ed. Madrid: Clásicos Castalia, 1996.

Homer. *The Odyssey.* Trans. Robert Fitzgerald. 1961. Reprint, Garden City, N.Y.: Anchor Books, 1963.

Las Casas, Bartolomé de. *The Devastation of the Indies: A Brief Account.* Trans. Herma Briffault. 1965. Reprint, Baltimore: Johns Hopkins University Press, 1992.

Mulcaster, Richard. *The First Part of the Elementarie.* 1582. Facsimile reprint, Menston, Yorkshire: Scolar Press, 1970.

Nebrija, Elio Antonio de. *Gramática castellana.* Ed. Miguel Ángel Esparza and Ramón Sarmiento. Madrid: Fundación Antonio de Nebrija, 1992.

Petrarca, Francesco. *Petrarch's "Africa."* Trans. Thomas G. Bergin and Alice S. Wilson. New Haven: Yale University Press, 1977.

———. *Petrarch's Lyric Poems: The "Rime Sparse" and Other Lyrics.* Ed. and trans. Robert M. Durling. Cambridge, Mass.: Harvard University Press, 1976.

Ronsard, Pierre de. *Œuvres complètes.* Ed. Gustave Cohen. 2 vols. Paris: Bibliothèque de la Pléiade, 1950.

Sandoval, Prudencio de. *Historia de la vida y hechos del emperador Carlos V.* 3 vols. Madrid: Ediciones Atlas, 1955–1956.

Sidney, Sir Philip. *An Apology for Poetry.* Ed. Geoffrey Shepherd and R. W. Maslen. Manchester: Manchester University Press, 2002.

Spenser, Edmund. *Poetical Works.* Ed. J. C. Smith and E. de Selincourt. 1912. Reprint, Oxford: Oxford University Press, 1970.

Speroni, Sperone. *Dialogo delle lingue (1542).* In Joachim du Bellay, *La Deffence et illustration de la langue françoyse,* ed. Jean-Charles Monferran, pp. 189–279. Geneva: Droz, 2001.

Tasso, Torquato. *Jerusalem Delivered.* Trans. Edward Fairfax. 1600. Reprint, New York: Capricorn Books, 1963.

Virgil. *The Aeneid.* Trans. Robert Fitzgerald. New York: Vintage Books, 1981.

———. *Virgil.* Ed. and trans. H. Rushton Fairclough. 2 vols. Loeb Classical Library. Cambridge, Mass.: Harvard University Press, 1978.

Secondary Works

Ascoli, Albert Russell. *Ariosto's Bitter Harmony: Crisis and Evasion in the Italian Renaissance.* Princeton, N.J.: Princeton University Press, 1987.

Asenio, Eugenio. "La lengua compañera del imperio: Historia de una idea de Nebrija en España y Portugal." *Revista de filología española* 43 (1960): 399–413.

Bernardo, Aldo S. *Petrarch, Scipio and the "Africa": The Birth of Humanism's Dream.* Baltimore: Johns Hopkins Press, 1962.

Bjaï, Denis. *La Franciade sur le métier: Ronsard et la pratique du poème héroïque.* Geneva: Droz, 2001.

Blockmans, Wim. *Emperor Charles V, 1500–1558.* London: Arnold, 2002.

Bono, Paolo, and M. Vittoria Tessitore. *Il mito di Didone: Avventure di una regina tra secoli e culture.* Milan: Edizioni Bruno Mondadori, 1998.

Burke, Peter. "The Image of Charles V: Construction and Interpretations." In *Charles V, 1500–1558, and His Time,* ed. Hugo Soly, 393–475. Antwerp: Mercatorfonds, 1999.

Calvo, Mariano. *Garcilaso de la Vega: Entre el Verso y la Espada.* Castilla-La Mancha: Servicio de la Publicaciones, 1992.

Chastel, André. *The Sack of Rome, 1527.* Trans. Beth Archer. Bollingen series 35.26. Princeton, N.J.: Princeton University Press, 1983.

Checa Cremades, Fernando. *Carlos V: La imagen del poder en el Renacimiento.* Madrid: Ediciones el Viso, 1999.

Cruz, Anne J. "Arms Versus Letters: The Poetics of War and the Career of the Poet in Early Modern Spain." In *European Literary Careers: The Author from Antiquity to the Renaissance,* ed. Patrick Cheney and Frederick A. de Armas, 186–205. Toronto: University of Toronto Press, 2002.

———. "Self-Fashioning in Spain: Garcilaso de la Vega." *Romantic Review* 83 (1992): 517–538.

Curtius, Ernst Robert. *European Literature and the Latin Middle Ages.* Trans. Willard R. Trask. 1953. Reprint, New York: Harper Torchbooks, 1963.

Darst, David H. *Juan Boscán.* Boston: Twayne, 1978.

Davies, R. Trevor. *The Golden Century of Spain, 1501–1621.* 1937; New York: Harper Torchbooks, 1965.

Diamond, Jared. *Collapse: How Societies Choose to Fail or Succeed.* New York: Viking, 2005.

———. *Guns, Germs, and Steel: The Fates of Human Societies.* 1997. Reprint, New York: W. W. Norton, 1999.

Ferguson, Margaret W. *Dido's Daughters: Literacy, Gender, and Empire in Early Modern England and France.* Chicago: University of Chicago Press, 2003.

Fernández Alvarez, Manuel. *Charles V: Elected Emperor and Hereditary Ruler.* Trans. J. A. Lalaguna. London: Thames and Hudson, 1975.

Fucilla, Joseph G. *Superbi colli e altri saggi.* Rome: Carucci Editore, 1963.

Gallego Morell, Antonio. *Garcilaso: Documentos completos.* Barcelona: Editorial Planeta, 1976.

Green, Otis H. *Spain and the Western Tradition: The Castilian Mind in Literature from El Cid to Calderón.* 4 vols. Madison: University of Wisconsin Press, 1963–1966.

Hadas, Moses. *A History of Latin Literature.* New York: Columbia University Press, 1952.

Haliczer, Stephen. *The Comuneros of Castile: The Forging of a Revolution, 1475–1521.* Madison: University of Wisconsin Press, 1981.

Heiple, Daniel L. *Garcilaso and the Italian Renaissance.* University Park: Pennsylvania State University Press, 1994.

Helgerson, Richard. *The Elizabethan Prodigals.* Berkeley: University of California Press, 1976.

———. *Forms of Nationhood: The Elizabethan Writing of England.* Chicago: University of Chicago Press, 1992.

———. *Self-Crowned Laureates: Spenser, Jonson, Milton, and the Literary System.* Berkeley: University of California Press, 1983.

Horn, Hendrik J. *Jan Cornelisz Vermeyen: Painter of Charles V and His Conquest of Tunis.* 2 vols. Doornspuk: Davaco, 1989.

Javitch, Daniel. *Proclaiming a Classic: The Canonization of "Orlando furioso."* Princeton, N.J.: Princeton University Press, 1991.

Keniston, Hayward. *Garcilaso de la Vega.* New York: Hispanic Society of America, 1922.

Kennedy, William J. *Authorizing Petrarch.* Ithaca, N.Y.: Cornell University Press, 1994.

———. *The Site of Petrarchism: Early Modern National Sentiment in Italy, France, and England.* Baltimore: Johns Hopkins University Press, 2003.

Lapesa, Rafael. *La trayectoria poética de Garcilaso.* 2nd ed. Madrid: Editorial Revista de Occidente, 1968.

Lida de Malkiel, Maria Rosa. *Dido en la literatura española: Su retrato y defensa.* London: Tamesis Books, 1974.

Lipking, Lawrence. *Abandoned Women and Poetic Tradition.* Chicago: University of Chicago Press, 1988.

Maravall, José Antonio. "Garcilaso: Entre la sociedad caballeresca y la utopia renacentista." In *Garcilaso,* ed. Victor García de la Concha, 7–47. Salamanca: Ediciones Universidad de Salamanca, 1986.

Marías, Fernando, et al. *Carlos V: Las armas y las letras.* Madrid: Sociedad Estatal para la Conmemoración de los Centenarios de Felipe II y Carlos V, 2000.

Menéndez y Pelayo, Marcelino. *Juan Boscán.* Madrid: Biblioteca Clásica, 1910.

Migliorini, Bruno. "La questione della lingua." In *Civiltà letteraria d'Italia,* ed. Vittoria Branca and Cesare Galimberti, 2:23–26. 3 vols. Florence: Sansoni, 1963.

Mignolo, Walter D. *The Darker Side of the Renaissance: Literacy, Territoriality, and Colonization.* Ann Arbor: University of Michigan Press, 1995.

Murrin, Michael. *History and Warfare in Renaissance Epic.* Chicago: University of Chicago Press, 1994.

Navarrete, Ignacio. *Orphans of Petrarch: Poetry and Theory in the Spanish Renaissance.* Berkeley: University of California Press, 1994.

Padrón, Ricardo. *The Spacious World: Cartography, Literature, and Empire in Early Modern Spain.* Chicago: University of Chicago Press, 2004.

Pagden, Anthony. *Lords of All the World: Ideologies of Empire in Spain, Britain and France, c. 1500–c. 1800.* New Haven: Yale University Press, 1995.

Parker, Geoffrey. "The Political World of Charles V." In *Charles V, 1500–1558, and His Time,* ed. Hugo Soly, 113–225. Antwerp: Mercatorfonds, 1999.

Quint, David. *Epic and Empire: Politics and Generic Form from Virgil to Milton.* Princeton, N.J.: Princeton University Press, 1993.

Rivers, Elias L. "El problema de los géneros neoclásicos y la poesía de Garcilaso." In *Garcilaso,* ed. Victor García de la Concha, 49–60. Salamanca: Ediciones Universidad de Salamanca, 1986.

Rodríguez García, José María. "*Epos delendum est:* The Subject of Carthage in Garcilaso's 'A Boscán' desde La Goleta.'" *Hispanic Review* 66 (1998): 151–170.

Seaver, Henry Latimer. *The Great Revolt in Castile: A Study of the Comunero Movement of 1520-1521.* Boston: Houghton Mifflin, 1928.

Seipal, Wilfred. *Kaiser Karl V. (1500–1558): Macht und Ohnmacht Europas.* Milan: Skira, 2000.

———. *Der Kriegszug Kaiser Karls V. gegen Tunis: Kartons und Tapisserien.* Milan: Skira, 2000.

Soly, Hugo, ed. *Charles V, 1500–1558, and His Time.* Antwerp: Mercatorfonds, 1999.

Strong, Roy. *Art and Power: Renaissance Festivals, 1450–1650*. Berkeley: University of California Press, 1984.

Tanner, Marie. *The Last Descendant of Aeneas: The Hapsburgs and the Mythic Image of the Emperor*. New Haven: Yale University Press, 1993.

Tracey, James D. *Emperor Charles V, Impresario of War: Campaign Strategy, International Finance, and Domestic Politics*. Cambridge: Cambridge University Press, 2002.

Vaquero Serrano, María Carmen. *Garcilaso: Poeta del amor, caballero de la guerra*. Madrid: Éditorial Espasa Calpe, 2002.

Weinberg, Bernard. *A History of Literary Criticism in the Italian Renaissance*. 2 vols. Chicago: University of Chicago Press, 1961.

Yates, Frances A. *The Art of Memory*. 1966. Reprint, Harmondsworth, Middlesex: Penguin Books, 1969.

———. *Astraea: The Imperial Theme in the Sixteenth Century*. London: Routledge and Kegan Paul, 1975.

———. *Giordano Bruno and the Hermetic Tradition*. 1964. Reprint, Chicago: University of Chicago Press, 1991.

Zimmermann, T. C. Price. "The Publication of Paolo Giovio's Histories: Charles V and the Revision of Book XXXIV." *La Bibliofilía* 74 (1972): 49–90.

Acknowledgments

This book owes its greatest debt to my research assistant William Gahan who for the last three summers has read with me through all of Garcilaso and large parts of Fernando de Herrera and the other early *comentaristas*. The translations in this volume are the product of his native Spanish with help from my experience as a regular visitor to the sixteenth century. In our translating, Bill and I have been aided by two other research assistants, Edward Test and Pavneet Aulakh, and by the careful review of two experts in the field, Barbara Fuchs and Jorge Checa. I also received welcome suggestions for the translation of Garcilaso's Latin from Sara Lindheim. I have further debts to the graduate and undergraduate students who have read Garcilaso and the other "new poets" of Italy, Spain, France, and England with me, especially to Simone Chess who came up with the idea on Garcilaso's feelings toward Boscán that I cite in chapter 6, and to a number of friends and colleagues who have read the manuscript either in whole or in part and have encouraged my work on it: Patricia Fumerton, Alan Liu, Elizabeth MacArthur, Michael O'Connell, William Warner, and my wife, Marie-Christine Helgerson, to whom the book is dedicated. The book also owes much to the unfailing support of its editor, Jerome E. Singerman, and to the painstaking editorial work of Noreen O'Connor-Abel and Jennifer Shenk.

My personal starting point with Garcilaso came with the happy purchase many years ago of Elias Rivers's wonderfully inviting 1966 bilingual collection *Renaissance and Baroque Poetry of Spain,* and I have since greatly profited from Rivers's two fine editions of Garcilaso, the *Obras completas* of 1974 and the *Poesías castellanas completas* of 1996. The discovery of Garcilaso through Rivers's editions has been aided by the work of many critics, a few of whom I would like to single out here: Anne J. Cruz, José María Rodríguez García, Daniel L. Heiple, and Ignacio Navarrete. Of these only Rodríguez García has devoted a full essay to the sonnet that is my subject, but both Heiple and Cruz have fine comments on it and both put it into a richly suggestive context. Though Navarrete does not discuss this poem, the value of his work on Garcilaso will be immediately evident to anyone familiar with the field. I have also gained much from Garcilaso's three most notable biographers, Hayward Keniston, María Carmen Vaquero Serrano, and Mariano Calvo. For reasons that stretch from a major computer glitch to the nature of the essay form, I have not included notes, but references to the work of these and the other scholars who have most contributed to my thinking will be found in the bibliography.

The prompting that turned a passive interest in Garcilaso and his moment into something more came from two invitations. As far back as 1997, Richard Kagan, Anthony Pagden, and their colleagues in the History Department at Johns Hopkins gave me a chance to extend to Spain and France some ideas I had developed on language and nationhood in England. More recently Megan Matchinske nudged me to give greater substance to these ideas with an invitation to present a three papers at the University of North Carolina, a performance that really meant Garcilaso could no longer be left as the poignant highlight that I had been making of him in other papers. Illness kept me from keeping the North Carolina date, but without that invitation and the welcome pressure it put on me I would not have been in position to begin writing this essay. Among the other papers, written and delivered between the Hopkins invitation and the one from Chapel Hill, have been discussions of one or another aspect of the "new poetry" at Sydney, Seattle, Irvine, the Huntington Library, Berkeley, Aberdeen, UCLA, Giessen, Santa Barbara, and Bermuda. Warm thanks belong to those who requested those papers and sat through them, and especially to those who asked to hear more.